WAR WITHOUT WEAPONS
Non-Violence in National Defense

Anders Boserup
Andrew Mack

SCHOCKEN BOOKS · NEW YORK

First SCHOCKEN edition 1975

Copyright © Anders Boserup and Andrew Mack 1974

Manufactured in the United States of America

Library of Congress Cataloging in Publication Data

Boserup, Anders.
  War without weapons.

  1. Strategy. 2. Military policy. 3. Nonviolence.
I. Mack, Andrew, joint author. II. Title.
U163.B63 1975   355.4'3   74-26920

CONTENTS

INTRODUCTION

Since the advent of nuclear weapons the use of military force for offensive as well as defensive purposes has become increasingly problematic and self-contradictory. Paradoxically, the construction of weapons with ever greater destructive power, occurring as it did on both sides of the Cold War front, in a formal sense increased the military might of each, but in a real sense decreased it. Both sides became exposed to the complete devastation which enemy attack or reprisal might bring: the genuine security and effective defence which the powerful had previously enjoyed had gone. With it went the ability of even the super powers to use their military might offensively in furtherance of their political aims. However perfect in a technological sense, modern weapons were increasingly useless as military instruments. In the early post-war years hopes therefore became fixed on the political changes which, so it was believed, nuclear weapons might bring in their wake. Some people had hoped that the West could retain a decisive military superiority — decisive in the sense of a strategic and hence a political supremacy — others that the threat of a common disaster would become the foundation on which a supra-national world order could be built. It is now clear that one hope was as vain as the other. When counting missiles or warheads, numerical superiority and primacy in sophistication do not translate into strategic supremacy, and in the shadow of the missiles, lesser wars could and did still go on, much as before. Yet, although patently a blind alley, the arms spiral continues, apparently endlessly.

Not leading as some believed they would to the creation of a political settlement in the form of a single — national (American) or international — predominant authority, the new weapons have had to assume the role which arms have traditionally held in a divided world, and in this role their performance is increasingly a failure. Few people are pacifist or anti-militarist as a matter of principle. Military preparedness and the use of force, even though distasteful to most, are not normally challenged and are indeed not without logic as long as they can further national policies and provide a defence policy. Increasingly they can do neither, and increasingly this is being realised. The emergence of the half-way pacifism of the campaigns for nuclear disarmament of the late fifties and early sixties, and, more recently, the powerful and still ongoing criticism of the military establishment, particularly in the United States, are there as evidence. Both movements have reached far beyond traditionally anti-militarist circles.

In this context the idea of providing for defence needs by the non-violent resistance of the population as a whole has gathered force. It appeared to be one possible way of effecting a radical break with policies which had locked the world in a sterile bipolar confrontation and an ever-expanding arms race; a break with strategic doctrines of 'peace by the threat of reciprocal destruction' which were increasingly seen as morally objectionable and faulty both in theory and in practice; and a break with military institutions which, in the name of defending freedom, were encroaching upon liberties at home, shoring up dictatorships abroad, and proliferating over all aspects of life, ultimately resulting in the creation of a warfare state in times of peace.

This idea of popular non-violent resistance is not new. Nor, of course, is its practice. In its current form, however, and as an explicit alternative to military defence it is on the whole a post-war development. The first thorough exposition and advocacy of this idea came in a book by a British writer, Commander Sir Stephen King-Hall, *Defence in the Nuclear Age*, which appeared in 1958 and articulated a 'tough', pragmatic approach to non-violence. Numerous articles and several monographs and readers have appeared since. This book is an attempt to survey that literature and to examine critically the proposals which have been put forward and the assumptions on which they rest.

Most people, inevitably, considered the call for non-violent defence as either downright subversive — an invitation to unilateral disarmament and to surrender without a fight — or else as a respectable idealism, but one that was hopelessly out of touch with reality. Some of the most publicised 'tactics' which have been recommended such as chaining people to bridges to prevent the passage of tanks, did not help to dispel the view that the proponents of non-violent defence — whether cunningly or unwittingly — were advocating a course which could only end in disaster. Yet recent events have shown that the idea at least deserves a fair hearing.

The war in Vietnam brought home several important lessons. First, it demonstrated the inadequacy and indecisive character of conventional military methods under certain circumstances, even where the supply of weapons and manpower was virtually limitless and the purely military superiority of one belligerent overwhelming. Second, it demonstrated that under suitable circumstances a strategy based on the political mobilisation of the people may hold in check and gradually exhaust a vast military machine. Third, and perhaps most important, it showed that the strategic confrontation need not be confined to the battlefield, but that under modern conditions and where protracted defensive warfare is concerned, the strategic space may be so expanded as to include the enemy home country — in this case the United States. The political and cultural constraints which are operative there and set certain limits to the forms and intensity of warfare which the enemy can conduct, can be exploited as a strategic resource, completely on a par with conventional resources such as firepower and advantageous terrain.

Ultimately, what all this has brought into question is the conventional wisdom that military force is the final and decisive recourse and arbiter of political confrontations between states. We have been reminded that the purpose of war is to affect the will of the enemy, and that to destroy his forces is merely a means to this end, sometimes necessary, sometimes not. By implication this has called into question the conception of the military as the nation's ultimate protector — which consequently ignores other possible defensive strategies. The virtually sacrosanct position above party politics which until recently the military enjoyed in most countries was a result of the unopposed sway of such notions. In the industrialised world we had reached a point where strategy was being equated with soldiers and trenches, and where we thought that this identity was imposed of necessity by the anarchic character of international politics. In fact this supposedly 'realistic' belief in military might is probably better described as the understandable illusion, the comfortable rationalisation of societies which, after a quarter century of peace, go on allocating a twentieth to a tenth of their total resources to military preparations. The policies derived from such beliefs may well work for a while — that is not in question — for a defence policy based on false assumptions will undoubtedly be effective (until tested in practice) provided these assumptions are shared by potential enemies. History is replete with *Maginot* lines which prove this. As we shall see the belief in the necessary pre-eminence of military force in defence policy results from a misconception of the strategic conditions of this age. The assumption that military force is best countered on its own terms had some validity in previous epochs. The self-contradictory character of 'nuclear strategies' comes from transposing this assumption to an age in which it is no longer valid and where a broadening of the sphere of strategic action has become necessary. At any rate, numerous examples, not least from World War II are there to show that a military defeat is merely the exhaustion of one among several means of defence. It may spell the end of resistance, but it need be no more than the transition from defence by the State to defence by the nation — from institutional to popular resistance.

As the Vietnam war became a demonstration that the military, in the traditional sense, cannot lay claim to a privileged position in an overall defence strategy, so the Czechoslovak resistance against the occupation by the Warsaw Pact countries in 1968 became a demonstration of the possible usefulness of non-violent techniques. In terms of its final outcomes, the Czechoslovak resistance was in many respects a complete failure. But this should not blind one to the considerable tactical successes of the first few weeks. The resistance vastly increased the practical difficulties and the political costs of the invasion. Significantly the Czech resistance was not destroyed by military force but by political manipulation.

Whereas it is possible to believe — rightly or wrongly — that guerrilla warfare as practiced in Vietnam can only be sustained in relatively undeveloped countries where nothing, short of complete extermination, can paralyse the countryside and uproot the resistance, Czechoslovakia in 1968 was a demonstration of non-military defence by an advanced industrialised society and under conditions of military inferiority, hardly less desperate than in Vietnam. Much of what the proponents of non-violent defence had advocated was being implemented in the first days and weeks of the Czechoslovak resistance. Overnight, a seemingly academic discussion had become real.

There is no general agreement in the literature on the scope of the concept of non-violence. In normal parlance violence is the intentional infliction of bodily harm, but many definitions have been used which are more comprehensive, for instance definitions which include 'psychic violence' such as provoking fear. Galtung (1965a) has tried to systematise a number of different definitions. None are more 'correct' than others, and many among the methods described below could quite reasonably be called violent if one were to adhere to a broad definition. It seems most meaningful in this work to retain a certain vagueness to the term, using it for actions which do not involve bloodshed but recognising also that its meaning is relative to established cultural patterns, that an action is not only non-violent by virtue of its intrinsic properties, but by virtue also of being performed in a situation in which more violent methods would normally be thought of as appropriate. For example a strike is not normally considered an instance of non-violent action (though, of course, it is not violent either), but when a strike is used during an occupation as a substitute for violent resistance it becomes a distinctly non-violent method. This way of using the term is all the more reasonable because it is generally claimed that one reason why non-violence 'works' is precisely that the action is less violent than the opponent would have expected.

The arguments advanced for non-violence are of two main types, here called 'ethical' and 'pragmatic'. In the former case violence is rejected on moral grounds, but apart from this it is difficult to find a common basis for this view as individual reasons for rejecting violence vary considerably. There is one group which holds that war and violence are in themselves morally unacceptable, whatever their purpose and form. This is argued in terms of religious beliefs or of a system of moral philosophy, i.e. of a conception of human nature and of Good and Evil. Another group rejects war, not *per se*, but because war – or modern war at any rate – fails to satisfy certain conditions which alone could have made it morally acceptable. In particular those who hold this view demand that the means used must be such as to be able to discriminate between combatants and civilians and that there must be a reasonable prospect that the war will lead to an improvement as compared with the pre-war situation. The Roman Catholic distinction between just and unjust war is of this kind. A third group, Sibley (1969), rejects violence on utilitarian grounds. Its members maintain that war always counteracts desirable political and social goals, whatever their short-term effects may appear to be, and whatever their declared purpose. This of course verges on a pragmatic position, since in this case the moral assumptions do not relate to war and violence as such but to the wider goals of policy, and whether these assumptions can be met by war is no longer a question of principle but a question of fact. Those who present their views in moral or religious terms often argue in utilitarian terms as well. Gandhi is an example of this.

Those whose line of argument is truly pragmatic, in the sense in which we use that word here would all agree with one or several of the above views – indeed most people would – but they add an argument of a completely different nature. They maintain that non-violence is (or can be made to be) more effective than military means, even when it comes to 'deciding' a conflict by defeating or expelling an occupant at minimum cost. They argue that even within its own narrow framework military defence is simply less effective than the alternative they propose. If this is so, then there is no argument at all to be made for military defence, and irrespective of the reasons one may have to prefer non-violence – and these are obviously weighty – the choice of a defence system can be made on technical grounds alone.

In addition to this form of the pragmatists' case for non-violent defence there is, as Schelling (1967) points out, a weaker form of the argument, also essentially pragmatic in character. According to it, non-violent defence is a useful device for putting pressure on the opponent and thus provides a stronger position from which to negotiate concessions. In this perspective, and barring other considerations, non-violent defence comes to appear as a useful addition to other means.

The pragmatic argument dominates most of the recent literature on civilian defence. As noted, this originated with King-Hall's *Defence in the Nuclear Age*. His pragmatic and 'tough' approach has on the whole been retained by later authors. Thus Ebert writes:

' . . . the major justification for non-violence is pragmatic . . . it is a sanction and a means of struggle which involves power . . . it does not depend on the assumption that man is inherently good.' (1967).

Here non-violence is seen as fulfilling the same functions as more conventional forms of defence. It is, in the words of another of its principal contemporary advocates, 'a functional equivalent of war' (Sharp, 1965).

These two forms of argument, ethical and pragmatic, are by no means contradictory — they rather complement one another — but they lead to quite different emphases, because they tend to relate to goals and to means respectively. In the former the main point is that what violence achieves (at best) is a decision as to who shall temporarily dominate whom, and this is not a 'solution' to conflict in any proper meaning, only a short-term postponement of *overt* conflict. Being totally unrelated to any concept of justice, this kind of conflict 'solving' is simply not a worthwhile goal. The pragmatic school, on the other hand, seeks to show that even if one were to adopt the traditional view of conflict according to which it is terminated ('solved') once a decision is reached on the battlefield, even then non-violence would be a more effective means of compulsion for achieving a decision which is to one's own advantage.

The pragmatic argument is therefore generally used in the context of a completely traditional view of the struggle which we here refer to as the 'negative' view of conflict to distinguish it from the 'positive' view which one often finds in the works which belong to the ethical school. These two views of conflict ultimately derive from entirely irreconcileable philosophies of conflict and their difference largely dictates corresponding differences in the means advocated. In the negative perspective a conflict is seen as a confrontation and a struggle for ascendancy of one group over another. The contenders have incompatible interests, and the enemy is opposed and fought with, even if by non-violent means. The emphasis is on raising the material and psychological costs to the opponent if he continues the struggle. The means advocated are strikes, boycotts, non-cooperation etc.

Adam Roberts summarises this approach to non-violent defence in the following terms:

'This policy is not aimed solely at changing the will of the opponent, it is also designed to make it impossible for him to achieve his objectives. Non-cooperation with the opponent's orders, obstruction of his actions, defiance in the face of his threats and his sanctions, attempts to encourage non-compliance amongst his troops and servants, and the creation of a parallel system of government, are among the methods which could be employed.' (1967a).

The main emphasis here is on thwarting the objectives of potential opponents through collective action in a social and political context of struggle. Non-violent methods are clearly seen as an instrument of power. There is not much emphasis on converting the opponent to one's views, and much more on forcing him. The positive view of conflict is more difficult to describe in its pure form, largely because we are unaccustomed to conceive of conflict in those terms. It affirms the oneness of the opponents in a wider perspective, so that the conflict is not seen as a confrontation between them, but rather as a problem, which they face in common, and which they face, so to speak, from the same side. In relation to the conflict they are not contenders but partners, and their oneness in this respect constitutes the possible foundation for transcending the conflict which — in a more superficial sense — divides them. In the Gandhian conflict philosophy, to which this conceptualisation owes much, the overriding unity of the contenders is held to be such that each, were he to comprehend the situation fully, would prefer an outcome which is desirable to his opponent, for he cannot fully realise his own self if he denies that realisation to others. In dealing with conflict Gandhi and his followers are led to emphasise trust, friendliness, fraternisation, limited cooperation, attempts to understand the views of the opponent, and the application of the same ethical norms to the opponent as to oneself.

To illustrate this one may draw an analogy, albeit only a partly valid one, between the Gandhian view of conflict and

14

certain conceptualisations of the relations of states in the age of nuclear overkill — witness Khrushchev's statement after the Cuban crisis (12 December 1962):

'Which of the two camps has triumphed, which has gained? One can say with certainty that it was good sense, the cause of peace and the security of the peoples which won.'

Here, evidently, the conflict is not seen as a contest between states but as a problem they *have* to transcend in common and which they *can* only transcend by mutual consent. It is of the interest of each to protect and assist the other. To see the situation as an antagonism between the superpowers is fundamentally a delusion. It is rather, to use the language of game theory, a kind of coalition against Nature. In another respect, however, the analogy is faulty, for in the Gandhian philosophy the oneness of the antagonists antedates any conflict between them, whereas in the 'philosophy' of nuclear terror it is a result of the struggle unto death in which they are locked and of the weapons they deploy, and would not arise if the threat of mutual annihilation had not been there. This philosophy of nuclear terror is more Hegelian than Gandhian.

While the positive view of conflict is frequently found in the literature on non-violence in general, it is exceptional in the post-war literature on civilian defence — i.e. on non-violence as specifically applied to national defence. Its major proponents in this latter context have been Bondurant and Naess. Nonetheless the works building on the positive perspective on conflict have had considerable influence on the mainstream of the literature on non-violent defence. In particular it has led to the inclusion in the latter of many typically 'positive' aspects, such as fraternisation and conversion, and to an emphasis on trust and openness which pervades much of this literature which otherwise clearly adopts a negative perspective on conflict. Galtung has been explicit in advocating a mixture of positive and negative means, and a philosophy which seeks to reconcile them. Occasionally this borrowing from the general literature on pacifism and non-violence has led to the adoption of the 'idealistic' perspective often found in the former, the tendency to conceive of the attitudes and moral strength of individuals as being the essential factors, rather than the social and political conditions which largely determine them. In this way considerable reliance is sometimes placed on psychological means of influencing the opponent and resistance tends to be reduced to a question of will.

The aim of this book is to present and to examine critically the proposals and underlying assumptions of the pragmatic school. It is thus assumed – incorrectly of course – that the sole purpose of non-violence is to be a more effective substitute for military defence. Therefore the conflict perspective adopted here is the negative one. Moreover, for reasons to be explained later, it seems to us that the methods which are characteristic of the positive view of conflict are difficult to reconcile with negative means. As a consequence this book is more inclined towards negative and pragmatic perspectives on non-violence than are most others.

The mode of presentation followed in this book is a combination of what might be called the 'analytic', 'casuistic' and 'theoretical' approaches.

In the *analytic* approach the various elements (means, methods, organisational forms, etc.) of non-violent defence are catalogued partly by drawing them from the imagination, and partly by 'abstracting' them from diverse historical cases of non-violent action (civil rights movements, industrial conflicts, popular resistance against occupation or military coups, oppositional activities in police states, and so forth). What can be achieved in this way is of course only to establish a catalogue of *conceivable* means, and only in that sense is this approach systematic. But it is necessary to go further. Some means may be mutually incompatible; others may reinforce and facilitate one another; particular means may make specific demands on the organisation of the resistance, the possibility of implementing them may be conditional upon the prevalence of particular social conditions, or they may have to be enacted in a particular temporal sequence. Sociological theory is so poorly developed that an attempt to take these necessary interrelations into account with its aid alone, would amount to almost pure speculation.

The *casuistic* approach attempts to get around the most glaring pitfalls of this kind by analysing specific historical occurrences. The purpose of the case studies included in this volume is not primarily to elaborate on particular means and methods, but to provide a modicum of information on the necessary interrelations between the different means and forms of non-violent defence, and on the way in which these elements are related to the wider social, political and historical context. In contrast, the value of historical case studies as illustrations of 'what might happen' is extremely limited. The parallels one may seek to draw between presumed 'historical precedents' and the unknown and largely hypothetical future cases of attack in which non-violent defence is meant to be enacted would be tenuous and entirely conjectural. The use of the specific occurrences of history as models for the future is no infrequent practice, but it leads one always to be prepared to fight the last war, and thus to be constitutionally unprepared to fight the next one.

The *theoretical* approach seeks to remedy this by distilling from the observation of past conflicts, not the 'things which happened', but the underlying 'laws of motion', the 'inner structure' which is common to all conflicts or to all wars, and which must therefore apply to future wars as well. Applying these laws to present social and political circumstances then enables one to construct from first principles and in crude outline what future wars may look like, and to develop strategies for dealing with them. In this, apparent similarity with precedents is not sought. On the contrary, similarity in structure despite wide differences in appearance is the surest indicator that one is on the right path. Properly analysed, the Napoleonic wars may in this way provide more valuable insights for developing the strategy of non-violent defence than the Czechoslovak resistance of 1968.

Chapter I is a rather abstract discussion of the relationship between positive and negative modes of conflict waging. It seeks to explain why the remainder of the book is almost exclusively devoted to non-violent resistance in the negative mode. The reason is that the two approaches are largely incompatible when they are used in group conflicts. They are so because the negative techniques ultimately depend for their effectiveness on polarisation, i.e. on the establishment of sharp boundaries between the antagonists and of strong cohesion among the defenders. Positive means, on the other hand, precisely depend on, and, to a considerable degree consist of, eradicating group boundaries and allowing for a large measure of independent and contradictory initiatives among the defenders. The conclusion is that in group

17

conflicts such as arise from attack and invasion, the negative approach must necessarily predominate.

The next four chapters deal with various aspects of the organisation of a non-violent defence. Chapter II takes up the various means, 'tactics' as they are often called, which have been proposed: strikes, boycotts, non-cooperation, and so forth. The aim is mainly to catalogue these means and organise them according to the functions they are supposed to fulfil. The chapter may be seen as a description of the available 'weapons' and of their modes of utilisation.

In terms of the same metaphor Chapter III deals with 'logistics' and with the defence organisation from 'platoon' to 'chiefs of staff' level. It takes up the questions of centralisation versus decentralisation, of open versus underground leadership and, more generally, of the coordination of the resistance.

Chapter IV seeks to draw certain parallels between guerrilla warfare and non-violent defence, i.e. it deals with those general features of non-violent defence which derive from its popular and civilian character (as opposed to the specialised and professional character of military defence). In particular it considers the functions of violence and non-violence in these two cases, the question of defence of social institutions rather than territory, and the specific conditions which the asymmetry of means between an attack which is military and a defence which is civilian imposes upon the form of the latter. This chapter thus sets the general limits within which a strategy of popular resistance must operate.

Finally, Chapter V considers the ability of the resistance to go on in the face of repression by the occupant. All too often this has been either skirted round or disposed of by reference to historic cases of heroic resistance. This is one of the clearest cases of the idealism (in the philosophical meaning) of much thinking on non-violence: heroic action and defiance in the face of repression are seen as a matter of will, of belief and of faith, and not of specific social conditions promoting these.

These five chapters complete the discussion of what is sometimes called 'internal defence', i.e. those actions which are implemented after an attack has taken place. The next two chapters return to these themes, but this time from the point of view of the case study. Four such cases are briefly examined:

two cases of resistance against foreign occupation (Chapter VI), and two of resistance against military coups (Chapter VII). Inevitably, these are sketchy and based on secondary sources. The aim each time is to trace those same aspects of non-violent resistance which were the subject matter of the first chapters, but this time to establish their mutual interaction. In this way the tentative remarks of previous chapters regarding the effectiveness of particular forms can be elaborated and based on firmer ground, since effectiveness is not an inherent property of a particular method, but depends entirely on the situation in which it is employed.

Chapter VIII is an extremely preliminary discussion of 'external defence', i.e. of the possibility that non-violent defence may be used, not only to thwart attack, but also to discourage or deter it in the first place. The chapter is no more than an attempt to identify where the problems lie. This discussion necessarily suffers from the ambiguities in argument and the conclusions which are well-known in the debates on nuclear deterrence. Both are indicative of fundamental inconsistencies in the 'deterrence theory', when it is used to *prescribe* action.

Chapter IX considers the several ways in which, *a priori*, non-violent and military means may be thought capable of being integrated into a common overall strategy. This chapter seeks to show that such a combination is in general worse than either 'pure' form of defence on its own.

In Chapter X, finally, non-violent defence is approached from the theoretical angle. The two perspectives adopted throughout this book, that of seeing conflict in the 'negative' terms of a struggle of opposed interests, and that of judging means on pragmatic rather than ethical grounds are the necessary and sufficient conditions for applying classical strategic theory to non-violent defence. This theory, due in all essentials to von Clausewitz, is at once *descriptive* in that it formulates the 'laws of motion' of war, and *prescriptive* in that it permits (in principle) to pass judgment on the effectiveness of different courses of action, different strategies in war. Since Clausewitzian theory (at its most abstract level) is directly applicable to non-violence, it enables one to determine the main features of a non-violent defence strategy. This in turn makes it possible to situate non-violent resistance in relation to alternative modes of defence –

WAR WITHOUT WEAPONS
such as military and guerrilla strategy — and to situate the various
methods of non-violent defence encountered in earlier chapters
in relation to an overall strategic conception.

CHAPTER I

Positive and Negative Conflict Behaviour: Theoretical Problems

1. POSITIVE AND NEGATIVE APPROACHES TO CONFLICT WAGING

Two diametrically opposed methods for achieving a goal through conflict, two opposite 'modes' of conflict behaviour, appear side by side in the literature and can be derived from it as abstract types. The purpose of this chapter is to contrast them more explicitly than has been done elsewhere, to compare their respective usefulness to civilian defence and to assess their compatibility in practical situations.

The mode which we call negative predominates among the pragmatic proponents of civilian defence, such as Sharp, Roberts and Ebert. Here the conflict is perceived as a struggle in the usual sense; compulsion and power are made use of when necessary, and civilian defence is seen as a 'functional equivalent of war' (Sharp, 1965). As appeals to the moral or human qualities of the opponent play a secondary role only, no particular assumptions about human nature need be made and no ethical or moral system is presupposed. For this reason it can be said that the pragmatic argument for this type of non-violent defence is the main one – the claim that it is simply the most effective means of defence. The other party to the conflict is seen as an opponent and the purpose of the struggle is to make him withdraw.

The 'positive' mode is most clearly formulated in Gandhi's work, but in the literature on civilian defence it is mostly Naess and Galtung who have advocated it. Here the idea is to seek mutually acceptable, rather than unilaterally imposed solutions, and therefore concepts like trust, truthfulness and openness play an important role. It is either implicitly assumed or explicitly stressed that certain assumptions are being made about the opponent; that if fear, misunderstanding, prejudice and mistrust can be removed the opponent will be accessible to reason and to moral appeals.

Gandhi builds upon such an assumption about the moral potential of the opponent and his susceptibility to reason. Action, in his view, should emphasise interests which the opponents share and should seek to resolve the oppositions between them by refusing to do harm (*ahimsa*). Compromise, on the other hand, that is to say the deflation of demands, should not be used, except in matters where no important principles are involved. In *satyagraha* it is assumed that a sense of justice can be awakened in the opponent. *Satyagraha* extends from rational persuasion, through self-imposed suffering, to non-cooperation and civil disobedience; the latter of which Gandhi sees as obedience towards higher moral laws. All these means are not to be understood as means for coercing the opponent into particular forms of behaviour such as capitulation, but as ways of helping him to understand what the conflict is actually about, of making him aware of one's own views and of the unjust character of his actions, and of making him consider the moral issues anew.

Despite the fact that they are often referred to as non-violent coercion, actions such as civil disobedience and non-cooperation therefore involve a form of coercion which is different from that which is implied when the same methods are used in a 'negative' campaign. Non-violent coercion, as this term was used by Case (1923), and, more recently, by Sharp (1965) and Lakey (1968) is characteristic of behaviour in the negative mode. For Lakey, non-violent coercion 'forces the opponent to accept the actor's demands even if he disagrees with them'. Galtung's 'negative influence techniques' are broadly similar in conception and are defined as 'increasing the probability that Alter (the opponent) refrains from actions negative to (i.e. undesired by) Ego (the actor)' (1965). In both cases it seems that the basic idea is to increase the actual and anticipated costs of the opponent, both material and psychological.

The 'positive influence techniques' serve to 'increase the probability that Alter performs actions positive to Ego' (*Ibid*) and according to Galtung they are characteristic of what we have called the positive approach to conflict. More important is what Sharp (1965), Lakey (1968), Galtung (1959) and many others call 'conversion'. Lakey defines it as 'winning the opponent to the point of view of the actor', while Galtung stresses that conversion strives after accepted, rather than imposed solutions, and involves a 'change of heart' in the opponent.

Strikes, boycotts, non-cooperation and so forth are normally seen as characteristic of the negative mode but, as we have pointed out, they may occasionally be used in the positive mode. Rewarding actions, active conciliation, fraternisation etc. are among the positive techniques most frequently advocated. Where the 'pragmatists' propose the use of such means their interest seems to lie, not so much in conversion of the opponent, but rather in reducing hostility levels and the risk of violent eruptions on the one hand, and, on the other, in promoting dissent and disaffection within the ranks of the opponent in order to weaken his power position. In other words, these techniques are used in this case mainly to force the opponent to withdraw.

The conclusion of these considerations must be that there is no one-to-one correspondence between the two modes of conflict waging on the one hand, and the means used on the other hand. Probably, it is precisely this ambiguity by which, according to circumstances, widely different intentions (and effects) may be associated with the same means, which, together with the widespread tendency to categorise means according to their outer manifestations (strike, boycott, etc.), leads to the conceptual confusion of the positive and negative modes which so often occurs in the literature.

Below we shall try to show why, in our opinion, the positive mode cannot hold a central place in a civilian defence policy. This is so essentially for two reasons. First, the large-scale use of these methods would presuppose a complete reorientation of the public's view of the opponent, which it seems unrealistic to expect, in case of an invasion. Secondly, such a change in attitudes, if it did take place, would break down the polarisation (i.e. the psychological climate and the organisational patterns associated with intense group conflict), which, as will be argued below, is precisely the prerequisite for the collective actions against the opponent which characterise the negative approach.

The importance and desirability of positive methods in other

WAR WITHOUT WEAPONS

contexts is not denied, and they have an obvious role to play in the prevention of conflict. Positive methods have also been used systematically in situations of intense conflict, but in these cases it seems to have been invariably the work of small groups of a sect-like character with a very high degree of internal discipline. In order to work in a situation of intense conflict these methods require a very high level of ideologisation, i.e. of belief in their ultimate effectiveness or moral necessity, and a high level of training, neither of which it is realistic to expect of the population of a modern industrial society.

However, there is no doubt that the work of the proponents of the positive methods, particularly that of Naess and Galtung, is extremely valuable in pointing to the dangers inherent in conflict polarisation and in suggesting means whereby these dangers may be diminished.

2. POSITIVE AND NEGATIVE MEANS OF INFLUENCE.

We have so far been suggesting that there is a certain parallelism between, on the one hand, the two modes of conducting conflict, and on the other, each of the two classifications of actions in conflict situations according to the way these actions function (but not according to their phenomenological manifestation). In this way means of non-violent coercion and Galtung's 'negative influence techniques' correspond to the negative mode, and *vice versa*. It is, however, necessary to consider this relation more carefully.

The difficulty with a classification system based on concepts such as 'conversion' and 'non-violent coercion' and the reason why they are ill suited for analytic purposes is on the one hand that this tends to lump together methods which have little in common, while others (for example 'bribery') get lost in the process, and on the other, that the categories remain ambiguous. Intuitively they seem to be meaningful (and they might therefore be useful for political purposes) because we tend to think of them in terms of examples which can be unambiguously classified [a number of such examples are given in Case (1923), Gregg (1960) and Sharp, (1973)], but there are as many examples of actions which cannot be unequivocally classified. In Case's system, for instance, the opponent may be either 'coerced' or 'converted' if his conscience is activated by the self-imposed suffering of the non-violent actors. If the suffering is deliberately self-inflicted with the aim of hitting the opponent's conscience, the process is called non-violent coercion, otherwise it is called conversion. Thus two apparently radically different categories turn out to be distinguished (in this case) only by what is believed to have been the intentions of the (non-violent) defenders. The confusion goes further than this. Lakey, as was noted, defined coercion and conversion in terms of the subjective experience of the object of the action ('Alter'), while we are now forced to consider the subjective experiences of the actor ('Ego') as well.

In a similar fashion Galtung's definition of positive and negative influence techniques is only unambiguous if one thinks in terms of certain obviously applicable examples of behaviour. But one may ask whether his categories are not just two sides of the same coin, since to cause the opponent to refrain from negative actions may also in itself be seen as a positive action. If, for example, the aim is to prevent the opponent from executing hostages, and if this succeeds, then it is a matter of taste whether to describe this as the opponent's abstention from a negative action (not executing) or as his performance of a positive action (granting a reprieve).

In addition to these attempts to classify methods according to the way in which they are supposed to function there is a large number of classifications based upon the manifestation (or appearance) of the actions. The most notable are those of Sharp (1959), Galtung (1959, 1965 and 1967), Case (1923) and its derivatives, Lakey (1962) and Sharp (1965), but we shall not consider them here, since non-violent methods are treated more fully in the next chapter.

The common starting point of most classificatory schemes seems to be the idea that it is meaningful to distinguish between positive and negative actions in the sense of the opposition friendly/hostile, and this distinction also seems to be linked in a natural way to the two conflict modes.

In the final analysis it is evident that a definition of positive and negative actions must be highly artificial if it is to give a clear-cut classification of all conceivable methods. Any given action has a number of features, each of which may be 'positive' when considered in isolation, but when taken together some may be positive and others negative. An action might be said to be completely positive if its effects are desired by the opponent, if the actor is aware of this and deliberately tries to achieve it, if the action has a positive effect on the mutual sentiments of both parties (i.e. if it increases the friendly dispositions of both), if the actor is aware of this and deliberately seeks to achieve it, if the action increases the likelihood that the opponent will react with positive, rather than negative behaviour, and so forth. Similarly it is clear what a completely negative action is. It is resented by the opponent, intended to hurt him, perceived as such by both parties, responded to in the same spirit, etc.

Only occasionally will it be possible to tell whether one action is more or less positive than another, because its several features might well be mutually contradictory: some positive, others negative, and yet others, entirely neutral (as in exchange relations). But it is nevertheless possible to conceive of a scale from positive to negative actions, i.e. of a certain possibility of comparing actions, as long as this scale is used to compare actions which differ in one of their features only.

There is no need to dwell upon this possibility of introducing a partial order in the set of isolated actions which may occur in a conflict situation, for at this point all we need to note is that it is possible to attach a meaning to the idea that certain alterations of an action will shift it in the direction of the positive or of the negative end of the scale. Indeed, the crucial point is not this, but the proposition that there is a tendency for clustering and contamination among the several features of an action, meaning that when one feature is positive there will be a tendency — other things being equal — for other features to be so too. A similar tendency is found in a *sequence* of actions taking place between two opponents. Positive actions will have a tendency to elicit positive responses and *vice versa* for negative actions. If, for instance, a negative feature is introduced in one of the actions of an otherwise positive sequence this will be perceived as dissonant in the given context and will perhaps be interpreted as a mistake. If, however, actions with negative features become recurrent the idea is that this will in the long run break down the positive interaction pattern and create a negative relationship instead.

In this way there is a certain stability at each end of the scale (the completely positive and completely negative action sequences), so that minor slips will be ignored and will have no lasting consequences. At the same time we have implied that it is possible in principle to shift a whole sequence towards the positive or the negative end by the systematic insertion of positive, (or negative), actions and features in the sequence.

Thus, in a sequence of negative actions, a single positive action by one of the parties is likely to be perceived negatively by the opponent and to be dismissed as a trick or viewed as subversion. The point would be, however, that this vicious circle can be broken by systematically introducing positive actions making the entire relationship between the parties more positive. This is, in broad outline, the idea behind the positive approach to conflicts. It leads to recommending the deliberate introduction of de-stabilising factors in a negative action sequence by acting with trust, openness etc. towards the opponent until the conflict itself vanishes, the entire action sequence having become positive.

It should be fairly clear by now that there are several important difficulties with this approach, although they may not be insuperable in all cases.

First, there is an evident tendency to reduce the conflict to its behavioural manifestations. It is incontestable that negative behaviour in conflicts impairs the search for solutions and, in most cases, adds additional substance to the conflict (for instance by the investment of prestige, or the question of war reparations), but in general there will be some conflict issues which are not caused by the conflict behaviour of the parties and existed prior to that behaviour. When this is so, one side may engage in actions which are intended to be positive and to be perceived by the opponent as positive. Even if the opponent does in fact so perceive them, his reaction may nevertheless be negative, simply because interests are contradictory.

Another problem arises from the above-mentioned stability of negative action sequences. Because of it, new positive actions will have to be introduced all the time to prevent a relapse. To effect this gradual transition from the negative to the positive mode is like swimming upstream in a river.

Finally, those who are to carry through this transition must have an unfailing belief in the eventual success of the method, and they must have the tenacity to persevere in spite of early experiences which must necessarily be discouraging. In fact this

27

approach presupposes an ability *not* to learn from experience, in other words, a dogmatic attitude based either on a long-term strategy which the whole group understands and endorses, or else on a considerable degree of indoctrination. In contrast, the negative approach can rely to a much greater extent on spontaneous and emotional reactions from case to case.

The foregoing analysis of positive and negative actions, of their tendency to self-amplification, and of the possibility of deliberate and gradual change from a negative to a positive action sequence finds its most straightforward applications in situations where the action sequences and the effective relationship between two individuals is unaffected by the broader social context within which they interact.

It is clear, however, that in the psychological climate following an occupation the social environment will exert a decisive influence upon the relationship between individuals on opposite sides in the conflict. If one could 'extract' one of the soldiers of the occupying force and one of the participants in the civilian defence effort from their respective contexts and let them interact with one another in complete isolation, it is not unreasonable to expect that the feelings of hostility as well as the more objective opposition between them could be broken down. In practice, of course, such an isolation is not feasible.

It is hard to escape the impression that wherever positive means (conversion, etc.) are recommended in the literature, the author is in fact thinking of such isolated pairs of individuals and ignoring the social and psychological context. It seems that the conversion of groups is never considered in the literature – it is always implicitly assumed that conversion of the opponent takes place on an individual basis. Two conceptualisations can be found. In one case it is the leader of the opposing group who is the target of conversion efforts, while no real effort is expended on the rank-and-file, so that this is again in effect a two-person conflict (as an illustration Gandhi's campaigns may be mentioned – see, for example, the letter to the Viceroy of India, prior to the 1930 civil disobedience campaign, reproduced in Gleditsch, 1965c). In the other case, conversion of the opponent is apparently conceived of as merely the sum of individual conversions.

The moment one considers two groups in interaction, rather than two individuals, a number of phenomena arise, which have no counterpart in the two-person case. An example is the 'contagion effect', the tendency towards the alignment of sentiment and behaviour within each group, i.e. the fact that individuals do not simply have an opinion to which they hold on until convinced of its falsity, but that they tend to join the bandwaggon when others change their opinions. In the next section we shall give a more thorough description of polarisation, i.e. of the psychological climate and the organisational structure within which interaction takes place in the case of *group* conflicts. This will also enable us to ascertain the extent to which the positive methods — the relevance and usefulness of which in most two-person situations is not contested — can be applied in group conflicts.

3. POLARISATION

The concept of polarisation refers to the way in which conflict groups are organised, the latter word being taken in its most general sense. Polarisation is, therefore, a property of the total system within which the conflict unfolds and in broad terms one might say that the more sharply differentiated and internally homogeneous the groups are, the more polarised is the system. Thus polarisation has no equivalent in two-person conflicts.

There are a number of different properties of a polarised situation, each of which could be used to define it. But, just as in the case of positive and negative actions considered above, this would mean putting a wholly arbitrary emphasis on particular features at the expense of others. It is, therefore, more reasonable to proceed as previously, only seeking to establish a partial ordering of situations according to the degree of polarisation. In this way one can again define the two ends of a scale unambiguously: the fully polarised and the fully de-polarised situations. But these end points, of course, never occur in practice. For those situations which one is likely to meet in reality, it will only be possible to compare those which differ in one property only. For our purposes, however, that will suffice.

In an intensely polarised situation group boundaries are sharply drawn: every individual belongs to one of the groups, and those who try to remain neutral are perceived as enemies by both sides. Attitudes, sentiments and behaviour are aligned within each group so that they both reflect and amplify the

29

division of the system, and so that cross-cutting conflicts between classes, religious denominations or other groups are superseded by the conflict with the out-group. Altogether the polarised situation is characterised by a general intolerance of dissent within the in-group, especially in regard to differences over goals and values. In this way the sharp external group boundaries are matched by a blurring of internal differences. Another property of a strongly polarised situation is the tendency to attribute stereotyped views to the opponent, frequently the direct opposites of one's own views and aims. Finally, there is a tendency for interaction between the groups to be strictly regulated, contacts being tolerated only when they are of a negative or hostile nature. All those forms of inter-group interaction, which normally take place without coordination and on the basis of individual initiatives are restricted; the interaction which is retained is formalised and routinised.

A de-polarised situation, on the other hand, is completely unstructured. There may be a conflict, but some individuals will not be taking part in it, others will hold that the conflict is relatively unimportant, and will differ over the really important issues. They may therefore be conducting their own cross-cutting battles. The boundary between the groups will be quite diffuse. Members of one group will be allowed intimate personal relationships with members of the other group, or a person may belong to one group or the other depending on the context (fraternising). Individuals who accept part of one group's doctrine while rejecting other parts of it are tolerated instead of being rejected altogether.

As in the case of positive and negative actions considered above, there is also a tendency towards alignment of the various properties associated with polarisation, because the occurrence of one facilitates the occurrence of others. It is clear, for instance, that the lack of contact between the groups, particularly the lack of private and personalised contacts, promotes conformity within each group, and that both of these factors tend to compel those who would otherwise have remained neutral to choose sides.

The degree of polarisation is an important property of group conflicts because, among others, it determines the ease with which positive or negative actions can be carried out. Moreover, the likelihood that a particular action will be perceived as positive or negative is itself dependent upon the degree of polarisation. Thus it will be more difficult to pull out of a negative action sequence the more polarised the situation is, and the negative sequence will itself contribute to increased polarisation.

It is also clear that polarisation facilitates collective action towards the opponent, if only because of the internal conformity it entails, and of the sharp distinction between 'we' and 'they'.

Thus the degree of polarisation is an overall measure of a set of characteristics of group conflict all of which tend to occur together. The greater the polarisation, the better the conditions for using the negative approach to conflict, and the less it is, the better the conditions for the positive approach. The reverse is also true: the use of the positive mode will tend to break down polarisation, and the use of the negative mode will strengthen it. And it is precisely these facts which make it difficult to use the negative and the positive approaches together. Furthermore, polarisation arises spontaneously in group conflicts and is even difficult to do without. One reason for this is that polarisation serves to protect the groups. Not only does it protect the individuals in each group but, more importantly, it safeguards the mutual trust, the cohesion and the solidarity within each group. Even if it had been possible to alter polarisation at will, so that one could arbitrarily improve the conditions for actions in the positive mode, this would have serious implications for the ability to continue the struggle. These problems will be considered in greater detail below.

4. POLARISATION AND THE POSITIVE METHODS

We have seen that in a conflict between two persons there do not appear to be any insuperable problems involved in shifting to a positive action sequence, and thus seeking a termination to the conflict using the positive approach. In a group conflict, however, the difficulties are much more formidable, and when the system is polarised individuals who try to use positive methods will be under pressure from *both* sides to make them follow the normal pattern and wage the conflict in the negative mode.

That point becomes evident when the consequences of using positive methods in a polarised situation are spelt out. Attempts to treat the opponent in a *genuinely* positive manner (and this, it

31

is claimed, is required if the methods are to work) will almost certainly be regarded with suspicion and, perhaps, fear by other members of the actor's own group, because it necessarily implies that the regulations about restrained and formalised contact between opponents must be violated. As will be stressed repeatedly in later chapters, the maintenance of group cohesion is probably the most important single factor determining the ability of the resistance to go on. But it is precisely this unity which is threatened when individuals are allowed to interact freely with the opponent, particularly if that interaction is of the positive kind. The suspicion must inevitably arise that individuals use their contacts with the opponent to secure a privileged position for themselves in case the resistance were to break down.

In addition to the functions they serve in a two-person conflict, the outward signs of hostility and rejection which accompany the use of negative methods have other important functions in a group conflict. An explicitly hostile attitude towards the opponent is a signal and a guarantee to the members of the in-group that solidarity is still maintained, and that no-one is trying to get on good terms with the enemy to save his own skin at the expense of others. Attempts to resort to the positive methods where this is generally seen as inappropriate, are, therefore, likely to cause apprehension and dissent and thus promote the disintegration of the resistance, because no-one wishes to be the last to jump off the bandwaggon. In general, every action which can be interpreted as collaboration is likely to cause dissent and precipitate the break-down of the resistance.

A similar situation may be expected to apply to the opponent. Initially, he is likely to interpret genuine overtures as tricks, and even if he does perceive them as genuine, he will hardly fail to notice that their effect can only be to create dissension and disaffection within his own ranks and thus undermine *his* group's unity. The most likely reaction of the opponent to positive actions is, therefore, to increase polarisation by restricting interaction, for instance by isolation of his troops or by substitution with troops who speak another language.

If used to any significant extent, the positive methods would thus create divisions on both sides of the conflict. This is of course a phenomenon which, by definition, can only occur in group conflicts, and the fact that such effects are hardly ever discussed by proponents of the positive approach is further evidence of the tendency to analyse the conflict as though it were a two-person conflict. It also demonstrates the difficulty with typologies derived from two-person conflicts which, like Galtung's positive and negative influence techniques and — even more so — the categories 'coercion' and 'conversion', are definable only in terms of the psychic correlates of actions. Although Galtung explicitly notes that the 'actors' in his typology may be groups or nations, and are not restricted to individuals, these groups and nations are nevertheless treated as though they were individuals, because (among others) the concepts nowhere take into account the problem of internal cohesion — in other words of the *existence* of a unit which performs the action. In its place one finds an implicit assumption about the existence of some sort of collective will.

It must be mentioned, however, that Galtung, apparently unlike any of the other authors in the field, is fully aware of the difficulties involved in using what he calls positive influence techniques in highly polarised situations. This and other reasons have led him to recommend that one should 'refuse to bow to the demands of conflict polarisation'. However, it seems to us that Galtung underestimates both the expediency, indeed the necessity of polarisation for the negative approach, and the problems, in an occupation situation, of gaining public acceptance for what he calls the 'de-polarised view of man'.

The usefulness of a high level of polarisation for conflict behaviour in the negative mode is fairly obvious. Polarisation is in fact the prerequisite of collective actions because it creates the national unity, the attitudinal alignment and the emotional foundation which are required for the success of actions such as strikes, boycotts and general non-cooperation. Unity and cohesion are maintained by transcending internal divisions through external strife, by limiting interaction between the groups to a minimum, and by facilitating internal control. Also the limited and formalised contact between the groups prevents the enemy from splitting the resistance by bribing particular groups. Civilian resistance, if it is to function in practice, presupposes a number of radical changes in public attitudes. This applies, in particular, to the attitudes to occupation. It is necessary that this be no longer equated with defeat, but instead be seen as the starting point of the real struggle. In an occupation the negative methods will be seen as appropriate since they still imply — as do conventional methods of defence — that one is engaged in conflict with a concrete enemy. Moreover, there are other experiences to draw on since civilian resistance is, in essence, a similar method to those which are used in other situations of intense conflict.

The positive approach to conflict waging presupposes far more radical changes in the way the conflict is conceptualised, so that, for example, the concept of 'enemy' itself disappears, or, at any rate, is given an entirely different meaning, one which is not normally associated with conflict situations at all, but rather with relationships characterised by trust, friendliness and co-operation.

Galtung, as we have seen, advocates a mixture of positive and negative methods and is — in contrast to other writers — fully aware of the difficulty in using both together. This leads him to ask how maximum positive contact with the opponent can be made compatible with minimum cooperation. His answer is to suggest that a distinction be made between the opponent and the confrontation, and that only the latter be fought. In other words, the idea is to distinguish the formal role of the opponent qua opponent, and his role as an individual human being. As an individual he is treated in a friendly manner, while he is confronted hostilely in his capacity as member of the occupying forces. By way of example Galtung mentions that the defenders may deny enemy troops the use of transport facilities, while at the same time inviting them home when they are off duty. There is, of course, already here a first difficulty in getting the population to make the same rather fine discriminations as the analyst. Furthermore, it seems to assume a considerable ability on behalf of each individual to alternate between positive and negative attitudes towards the same person or, instead, an ability to participate in the conflict, both positively and negatively, without involving his feelings. When it comes to group conflict it might be added that Galtung presupposes a greater measure of individual initiative in using positive actions than other parties in the conflict are likely to feel safe with.

For reasons which are easily understood polarisation tends to arise spontaneously in situations of intense group conflict. Without the need for manipulation from above or for previous instructions or training it is likely to arise as an inevitable consequence of foreign occupation. It is the foundation for collective acts, particularly of a negative kind, while at the same time it protects both groups against internal and external threats alike. The policy Galtung advocates, which consists in using positive methods to a considerable extent and at the same time promoting an ideology of depolarisation does not have these advantages. It presupposes an orientation to the opponent, demanding what seems to us to be an unrealistically high level of training, education and determination to achieve and to maintain, in the face of as unequivocally hostile an act as the invasion of an unarmed country. The use on a large scale of the positive approach in so intense a conflict presupposes the reversal of so many spontaneously occurring processes that simply to refer the problem to the need to 'refuse to bow to the demands of conflict polarisation' does not amount to a prescription, but is only a restatement of the problem. It is even a doubtful restatement because group behaviour of the kind and scale implied is unlikely to be a matter of collective will in any but the most limited sense. As far as we can see the problem of how to achieve this depolarisation is completely unanswered.

5. SUMMARY

We have tried here to clarify the distinction between the negative and positive approaches to behaviour in conflict. Very briefly it can be said that the first consists in waging conflict in the habitual way — except for the fact that the use of violence is avoided — while the second consists in converting the opponent to one's own position, emphasising or creating areas of common interest etc. Much of the existing literature refers now to one, now to the other, without making any clear distinction between these two modes. With a few authors, however, one does find an express advocacy of a particular policy — Naess in favour of the positive approach and Galtung of a combination of both.

Hence the need for making explicit the reasons why our presentation is based on the view that the positive methods must necessarily hold a relatively minor position in a civilian defence system.

The reason why the two approaches seem to us to be difficult to reconcile, and why the positive approach seems difficult to apply is that they are so closely linked to the degree of polarisation. Polarisation in group conflict seems to embody fundamental protective mechanisms which would be jeopardised if the positive mode were resorted to, and there are reasons to believe that the large scale use of positive methods would lead to the break-down of the resistance because internal solidarity could not be maintained.

These are theoretical arguments, but there is also a more practical argument: use of the positive methods would presuppose considerable changes in the public view of what constitutes 'adequate' conflict behaviour in an occupation.

In what has been said, no critique is implied of those theories or notions of a *psychological* nature upon which the assumption about the possible usefulness of the positive methods rests, i.e. of the assumptions behind their use in two-person conflicts. That would also have contradicted all our experience with conflict behaviour among individuals and in small groups where the positive methods evidently play a much greater role than the negative methods. The real problem arises, not with the psychological but with the sociological assumptions and in the literature one finds no indication of how positive methods are to be applied to group conflicts. To the extent that group conflicts are only described at the micro level, i.e. as composed of a large number of two-person conflicts, the problem, of course, does not arise, but without a macro description one can neither develop a strategy of the conflict situation as a whole, nor estimate the overall effects, feasibility or suitability of the micro level methods.

It should finally be stressed that while the arguments for attributing to the positive methods a *central* role in civilian defence against occupation do not seem convincing, this does not imply that these methods have no role to play. Quite the contrary is the case. The positive methods must undoubtedly constitute the main part of the preventive side of the defence — what we have called external defence — and they might be used during occupation to deliberately limit polarisation and control its harmful effects.

CHAPTER II

The Methods of Civilian Defence

1. OVERVIEW

A very large part of the literature on civilian defence is taken up by descriptions of particular methods and tactics used in past non-violent campaigns. Gene Sharp's *Politics of Non-Violent Action* and his *Defence Without War* include exhaustive lists and classifications of such historical precedents. In addition to this source other authors have used a more analytic approach, and have sought to derive prescriptions for new tactics or new combinations of tactics from abstract reasoning. A substantial part of the pacifist literature is of this kind, Galtung's work being perhaps the clearest example. While the former approach can be criticised for laying undue emphasis on the past, which constrains thinking too much and does not sufficiently take account of social, political, economic and technological changes, the latter, more theoretical approach, does not provide much guidance as to the practicability and, if practiced, the effectiveness of the methods advocated.

It seems that all the methods proposed for making the occupier give up and leave the country are of either of two kinds: those activities which aim at preventing him from achieving his initial objectives (various kinds of sabotage and non-cooperation), and those which aim at undermining his ability to continue the fight, whether this is done by converting him to the views of the defenders, by creating schisms within his ranks or by causing other powers to exert pressure upon him. In other words these activities serve respectively to decrease the direct benefits from occupation and to increase the costs of occupation, directly or indirectly. Many of the types of tactics considered (such as

37

strikes for instance) might of course serve several of these functions at once or they may serve different functions in different contexts.

There is, however, a third function which the tactical means discussed in the literature may serve and which does not directly affect the opponent's willingness or ability to persevere, but which instead provides the psychological basis for the resistance by promoting unity and sustaining the willingness to fight on. This we refer to as the symbolic function of a tactical means, and means which serve this function alone are referred to as symbolic activities. These we consider first.

2. SYMBOLIC ACTIVITIES: THE CREATION OF UNITY

Nearly all civilian defence writers emphasise the importance of symbolic activities such as demonstrations, protest marches, protest strikes, vigils, etc. — especially in the first stages of the resistance. Symbolic activities are largely affective acts of resistance from the point of view of the individual participants but they have a wider function for the resistance as a whole. This function is two-fold: first to demonstrate the unity and strength of the resistance both to its own members and to the opponent and, second, to delimit the resistance group and hence force dissenters and the non-committed to take a stand either for or against. Thus these symbolic activities serve to define the resistance as a moral community which may then provide a powerful basis for sanctions such as ostracism or social boycott (isolation) of dissenters, collaborators, etc.

For a number of reasons it is essential to have as wide a support as possible for the resistance movement, which is to say that the *active* resistance must be able to depend on at least *passive* support, and preferably active moral and material support, from the quasi-totality of the population. This passive support — or, at the very least, the absence of active support for the opponent — is widely recognised as being essential for guerrilla movements in providing protection, the means of subsistence, information, and so forth. In the case of civilian resistance, popular support plays an even greater role because a number of the non-cooperation techniques envisaged require the direct participation of the population.

Under the tense conditions of an occupation the main factors determining recruitment to, or dissaffection from, the resistance are probably twofold as far as the least ideologised section of the population is concerned: one is whether it is association with the resistance or with the occupying forces which is perceived as providing the greatest measure of peisonal protection; the other is the extent to which cooperation with the occupying power entails moral condemnation by, and isolation from, those face-to-face groups which an individual belongs to (family, circle of friends, work-mates,etc.), and whether it is consistent with the behaviour and norms of those persons, groups and organisations he normally seeks to emulate or otherwise uses as points of reference and as political and moral standards. The effectiveness oi each of these factors clearly presupposes that the resistance has quasi-unanimous support.

Thus the wearing of a paper clip by Norwegian civilians during the German occupation served not only, or not even primarily, to express personal feelings of protest — a so-called 'expressive' activity because it only aims at relieving personal tension. It was first of all a *social* activity serving as a signal of mutual support among the wearers and — to the extent that the practice would be widespread enough — as a signal to the non-committed that he would run the risk of social isolation if he collaborated with the occupant. Similarly, a demonstration of unity such as, for instance, a general strike will not only bring out those who already favour the resistance but will function as a bandwaggon in making many previously uncommitted join, and it will do so the more effectively, the more numerous and visible those who have already joined. It is, however, evidently a two-edged weapon: if too little support is achieved in the first place this demonstration of lack of unity and support may cause massive disaffection from the ranks of the resistance.

When properly used, social pressure of the kind discussed above can be an extremely powerful factor in welding together the resistance as became clear in the first days of the Czech resistance when it was impossible for the occupying countries to find anyone among the political leaders who were willing to join a collaborationist government or, for that matter, to get anyone to cooperate in any way. These events demonstrated that unanimous and coordinated action by the whole of the population is in fact a possibility. It would be naive to assume that no one in

Czechoslovakia held dissenting views from those of the majority, and the important conclusion is precisely that complete unity in action was achieved *in spite of* possible differences in views.

3. DENIAL ACTIVITIES: FRUSTRATION OF THE OCCUPIER'S AIMS

Below we shall consider, first, the methods of obstruction and sabotage, and then the different types of non-cooperation which have been proposed.

a) Physical Obstruction and Sabotage

Delaying the enemy advance: Physical obstruction and sabotage can play an important role in the first stages of defence against invasion, and this is so for several reasons:

First this serves to gain some time in which to make the necessary last minute preparations, deciding on which types of strategy to adopt, destroying files and records, establishing underground communications and administration, issuing instructions to resistance groups and so forth. This time aspect would seem essential however well the resistance had been prepared in advance, and many of these preparations would be much harder to make after the occupant had taken over.

The initial resistance also serves to dramatise the invasion and subsequent occupation both at home and abroad and thus stiffens resistance and arouses foreign sympathies. This is an activity for which control over the normal mass media is particularly important because so much depends on the widest possible communication of resolve and unity. Moreover, the very fact of retaining control, full or in part, of key institutions and institutions which have the character of national symbols signals the initial successes of the resistance and helps to radicalise opinion. In the first week after the invasion of Czechoslovakia the 'free Czech radio' had a crucial symbolic role of this kind (in addition to its many other functions).

On the other hand it does not seem possible to make obstruction and sabotage so effective that they amount to a border defence and actually arrest an invasion by an even minimally determined opponent. Nor would it be desirable to try to maintain the struggle at the level of border defence since this is the situation in which the defence is relatively the weakest. As already mentioned, the opportunity to influence the morale or the beliefs and attitudes of the opponent and to implement effective non-cooperation arises only after the invader has become an occupier. This is the important phase of the struggle, and whatever is done during the phase of invasion should be designed with a view to facilitating this later struggle, not as a substitute for it.

It is, therefore, clear that if one envisages a border defence based on obstruction and sabotage then this should be publicised as serving merely to *delay*, not to *prevent* invasion. It evidently makes a great deal of difference to the morale of the defence in its subsequent operations whether occupation is seen as the consequence of an initial defeat or as the beginning of a yet undecided and potentially successful struggle.

Obstruction: human and material: The placing of unarmed civilians in the path of a military advance is a method popularly associated with non-violent defence but it is one which has been advocated, rather than practised in the past and many authors have opposed it. In 1931 Gandhi suggested that Switzerland might be defended by a 'living wall' of men, women and children obstructing the frontiers, over whose corpses the opponent would have to pass in order to gain an entry (Gandhi, 1931, quoted in Roberts, 1967b). Others, realising that the physical removal of the 'living wall' was an obvious option for the opponent have suggested chaining people together in lines across bridges and railway tracks, mass 'lie-ins' on airfield runways and similar things. The hope is that the basic humanitarian attitudes of the opponent will prevent him from simply driving over the living bodies (which also provide a realistic *physical* obstruction in the case of airfield runways). If the opponent disregarded humanitarian considerations and simply went ahead, the moral outrage his acts would incur would, it is argued, rebound to his disadvantage. Again, there are obvious ways around it for the invader, including the simple removal of the people without harming them. This, however, would take time — which is the object of the exercise.

It cannot be doubted that in theory some time might be gained in this way, but it is at best a delaying tactic, not a means of denial. It is the implementation of a 'living wall' in practice which raises real problems, partly because these activities are generally conceived of as somewhat bizarre and are associated in the public mind with more or less eccentric sects. This is to say nothing of the risks involved and of the dubious morality of using human beings to block tanks.

If, instead, a military advance is delayed by obstruction with material objects or by destruction of transportation facilities these reservations no longer apply, but the moral coercion effect claimed of the 'living wall' approach is also lost. One possibility is to destroy facilities which would otherwise aid the advance of the invader such as bridges, ferries, tunnels and railways. Sharp (1965) suggests blocking roads with hundreds of abandoned vehicles, a technique which could also be employed for temporary blocking of airfield runways, railway tracks, etc., or — by sinking ships across the entrance — with harbours. Yet another approach is a more indirect obstruction; the clearest examples of which are to be found in the initial stages of the Czech resistance to the Warsaw Pact invasion. Street names and signposts were removed, trains were re-routed away from their destinations etc. Reportedly, some trains finished up again on the Soviet border after long excursions into the Czech countryside.

Evidently measures like those considered here can do no more than delay an invasion, and the effective onset of occupation, by a few hours or days. If considered in isolation, each device can easily be defeated but taken together they would seem to have a not inconsiderable effect.

As long as this obstruction is limited to the initial stages of an invasion and is carried out in a carefully planned, rather than a haphazard way, it seems unlikely that it would lead to severe reprisals or cause escalation into violence; but if obstruction of transport and similar actions are used systematically during occupation there is the problem that it may well hurt the residents more than the occupiers. This is what happened in the Ruhrkampf because the occupiers retaliated in kind, prohibiting all transport after the resistance had stopped specific shipments.

Sabotage: Sabotage may be directed against the military, the administrative or the exploitative potential of the opponent. In terms of physical targets the first will normally involve the opponent's property while the latter two generally involve the destruction of the property of the occupied peoples.

Sabotage against the opponent's property, and in particular against his military forces is condemned by most advocates of civilian defence both on moral and on pragmatic grounds.

In general it can be assumed that sabotage has little effect on the opponent's military capability. Commenting on the guerrilla/sabotage actions during the last war Liddell Hart says:

'The armed resistance forces undoubtedly imposed a considerable strain on the Germans [and] proved a serious menace to the German communications in Eastern Europe and the Balkans . . . [the German commanders] were acutely conscious of the worry and burden of coping with guerrilla foes who struck out of the blue and were shielded by the population.'

'But when these back area campaigns were analysed, it would seem that their effect was largely in proportion to the extent to which they were combined with the operations of a strong regular army that was engaging the enemy's front, and drawing off his reserves. [Otherwise] they rarely became more than a nuisance' (1967).

Sternstein makes a similar point about violent sabotage in the later stages of the Ruhrkampf:

'Arguments about violent sabotage upset the unity of the occupied area, achieved in the moral struggle of passive resistance. [The sabotage] had been of little effect, and hardly interrupted the lines of communication of the occupying forces to France and Belgium at all ' (1967).

Sabotage against enemy property necessarily involves a risk of loss of lives (on both sides) and this is particularly true of violent sabotage such as exploding installations, derailing trains etc. The loss of lives and the fear amongst the occupying forces as they come to feel themselves endangered serve on the one hand to justify increasingly violent repressive and retaliatory measures, and on the other hand to inhibit whatever moral restraints individual soldiers may otherwise have had against countering non-violence with violence. As Liddell Hart puts it, violence affords the enemy troops 'the opportunity for violent action that is always a relief to the nerves of a garrison in an unfriendly country ' (1967). The fact that opponents often welcome and try to provoke violent resistance from a generally non-violent movement is in itself a warning against actions which, like sabotage easily lead to violence, even though such is not their aim. The frequent use in the past of violent 'agents provocateurs' underlines this point.

Sabotage of one's own property involves considerably less risk of degenerating into violence and is less likely to upset the unity of the occupied, to reverse world sympathy and so forth. It may involve the destruction of information, records, etc., or of production and distribution facilities. In addition, as we shall see later, this type of sabotage facilitates non-cooperation activities in general and nullifies some of the conceivable reasons for invasion (such as gaining access to economic resources).

The problem that by destroying the systems of administration, production, distribution and communication these are denied the civilian population as well as the opponent (and the latter has easier access to outside substitutes) is common to all denial activities and it is one to which no simple solution can be suggested in the abstract. One may note, however, the possibility of establishing 'parallel' but less vulnerable structures underground (which is a particularly obvious solution for communications) and the possibility of limiting sabotage of, say, factories to the removal of certain parts which are difficult to replace instead of destroying the complete factory.

b) Non-Cooperation

While all authors agree that non-cooperation should be an important part of resistance to occupation there is some divergence as regards the forms it should take. Below, the main suggestions are briefly reviewed.

Total non-cooperation: Gene Sharp (1965) advocates total non-cooperation following an initial stage of symbolic resistance designed to communicate unity and firmness. He argues, however, that total non-cooperation might simply be a stage in the resistance struggle — a non-violent *blitzkrieg* which would include a general strike. Because total non-cooperation would be too costly to the population in the long run he proposes to switch to selective resistance aimed at a few key sectors and with a longer time perspective if the total non-cooperation fails to achieve its ends rapidly.

Probably the most extreme form of non-cooperation is the

proposal by J. W. Hughan (1942) that all public officials should be pledged to die rather than retreat from unconditional non-violent non-cooperation. Apart from the fact that such total and automatic resistance does not seem to be the best course under all imaginable circumstances, the proposal also seems difficult to enforce.

Working on without collaboration: Theodor Ebert (1967) advocates that the resistance should 'refuse to recognise the usurper's legality and to obey his orders . . . In general the emphasis should be more on a determined continuation of the existing social and political system than on resignations or strikes.' In other words Ebert would not *initiate* a 'non-violent *Blitzkrieg*' like Sharp's although there would be total refusal to cooperate with the opponent. The idea is that the legitimate holder of each particular post continues to work normally though absolutely refusing to obey any orders from the occupying power until removed physically from his post. If that happens, subordinates would take over and similarly refuse to comply with the illegitimate instructions of the occupier. Ebert argues that if officials stay at their posts instead of going on strike it will be more difficult for collaborationists to take over.

Resistance at key points or over key issues: This approach is advocated by Naess and King-Hall (1958). The difference between Naess and Ebert is one of emphasis but is important. Whereas in the previous case all orders from the occupying power are refused on principle this is not the case with Naess' approach where the ultimate aim is seen as defending the 'life-style of individuals' and the defence of institutions, which Ebert emphasises, is seen as contributing to this principal aim only indirectly. Naess's basic aim is to change the attitudes of the opponent rather than simply blocking the opponent's objectives by refusal to cooperate. The refusal on principle to cooperate with the opponent over issues which do not directly threaten the life styles of individuals is seen as being likely to alienate and antagonise the opponent unnecessarily and make it more difficult to convert him. Naess gives as an example the device used by some in the Norwegian resistance of immobilising German vehicles by putting sugar in the fuel tanks. This did nothing to directly safeguard the way of life

45

of the Norwegian civilian population, indeed it entailed the danger of reprisals, and on the other hand it made the 'active conciliation' methods designed to promote conversion much more difficult.

Perhaps Naess' approach should not be classified as a denial activity at all, since although non-cooperation is involved this is a secondary rather than a primary aim. Sharp's emphasis, on the other hand, on resistance at key points during a later and protracted phase of the conflict is clearly aimed at denial, seeking to block the opponent's attempts to undermine such institutions as a free press, 'the independent social groups and institutions of a democratic society,' etc.

Two other approaches to non-cooperation should finally be mentioned although they are perhaps best described as means for facilitating non-cooperation. One consists in claiming inability to perform a particular task, and the other in effectively preventing oneself from performing it by pre-emptive sabotage. In either case the ability of the occupier to enforce compliance is reduced.

"Schweikism" and "go-slow": The term 'Schweikism' derives from Jaroslav Hašek's novel about the Good Soldier Schweik who was 'dedicated to the low ideal of survival'. He did not *refuse* to cooperate, rather he showed an apparent willingness to cooperate coupled with an apparent inability to comprehend instructions properly or to carry them out. In 1968 the Czechoslovaks were apparently using the Schweik tactics of passive resistance and 'go-slow' very deliberately. The delays in the passage across Czechoslovakia of a train loaded with radio jamming equipment which was to silence the Czech 'free radio' provides a good example. There was no explicit refusal to obey orders (contrast Ebert's proposed 'work on without collaboration') but a long series of 'mistakes' and 'communication failures' which delayed the train for days until the occupying forces eventually airlifted the required equipment in.

Sabotage of property and institutions: All the tactics thus far discussed depend upon the ability of the resistance to withstand pressures and repression from the opponent to force compliance. Galtung (1967) proposes to depend less on the ability of individuals or groups to refuse cooperation and instead to make cooperation impossible for them. This approach has parallels with the 'scorched earth' tactics of military strategy, the emphasis being on the sabotage of property and social institutions. Galtung notes of sabotage against one's own property that the idea is to 'remove the minimum part which could cause the maximum uselessness'. This has fairly obvious applications for means of transport and communication, for factories and so forth. Apparently the Swiss made preparations during the last war for undermining over a hundred factories in case of German occupation and had trained a corps of 1600 saboteurs for this purpose (Gleditsch, 1965a, quoting Kimche, 1961). Of more general relevance to the other tactics discussed would be the destruction of central records, census data, occupational data and information on political affiliations. A copy of the records could be stored in advance abroad.

Galtung argues that the same principle would also apply to the social order as to physical objects. Here the idea would again be to 'paralyse the minimum part of one's own social order which would cause the maximum uselessness.' This would imply the removal of the most indispensable and irreplaceable actors in various sectors of the society. The experience of the Allied Powers in setting up a post-war administration in Germany and the necessity to assign many ex-Nazis to top positions because other qualified persons were lacking might illustrate this.

With regard to public administration during occupation the approach would consist on the one hand in rendering useless the existing facilities, including files (see also Ruge, 1965) so that non-cooperation does not rely on the continued willingness to resist to quite the same extent, and, on the other, in the removal of the most indispensable and irreplaceable individuals. Ebert's concern that strikes and non-attendance at work leave the way open to collaborators is less important here due to the presumed difficulties of finding others who could take over.

4. UNDERMINING ACTIVITIES: SPLITTING AND WEAKENING THE OPPONENT

As has been mentioned previously there is little to be gained and much to be lost by sabotage and obstruction against the forces of the occupier. What we are discussing in this section is, therefore, not the undermining of the physical military capability of the opponent but the undermining of his political ability to continue the occupation. While non-cooperation is directed primarily towards controlling the opponent's behaviour, the activities considered here operate primarily on the level of his attitudes.

The overall strength of the opponent may in particular be undermined by: (a) causing disaffection and dissent among the occupying forces; (b) causing disaffection and dissent in the opponent's home country or among his allies; and (c) mobilising other external forces against the opponent, or otherwise increasing his costs at the international level.

Many among the activities considered under the heading of denial activities may have the additional effect of undermining the opponent's strength in one or several of these ways but some approaches are designed expressly to have these effects. They include activities aimed at converting the opponent and appeals to his conscience and empathy. In the literature the main emphasis has been on affecting the occupying forces — because it is to these that the resistance has most direct access — but it is not evident that these are always the most effective targets to aim for.

a) Conversion

The emphasis on converting the opponent to one's own view is characteristic of the ethical pacifist approach to defence, whereas in the more recent literature on civilian defence conversion is much less emphasised. In the latter it is also treated rather more as a means towards weakening the enemy than as an end in itself.

It has been often emphasised that non-violent defence is particularly well suited for attempts at converting the opponent because the asymmetry between the positions of the attacker and the defender is such as to sensitise people to see the situation from the point of view of the defence. With a fully non-military and non-violent resistance the problem of identifying the aggressor or initiator of hostilities does not arise, particularly since the nation practising non-violent defence does not transgress the boundaries of its own territory (whereas a military defence, however 'defensively' its tasks may have been defined, will often need to conduct offensive actions in enemy territory). Numerous examples from recent history show that (other things being equal) world opinion tends to favour the smaller and weaker of two nations in conflict, the one whose methods are least brutal, the one which was attacked in the first place (when this can be ascertained) and the occupied rather than the occupier. The importance of this factor is illustrated by the widespread tendency in the propaganda of nations at war to slant their case in this direction, and since in the case we are considering the odium is so clearly placed with the occupant there is an evident initial advantage here.

It does not follow from this that anything like conversion will necessarily occur in practice, and conversion is evidently more likely to affect third parties to the conflict than the opponent himself. Furthermore, the claim is justified that so-called 'totalitarian' states are less accessible to undermining by conversion because of censorship, and that these countries, even if large sectors of the population were to oppose the policies of their government, this would have little effect in practice. Nevertheless, the importance of this point is often exaggerated. Disaffection did occur among the Soviet troops in Hungary in 1956 (see *United Nations*, 1957) and in Czechoslovakia the replacement of occupying troops from Eastern Europe by troops from the Soviet Far East with whom the population could not communicate so easily was apparently motivated by this problem of disaffection and loss of morale.

Sternstein (1968) explicitly turns against the 'myth of the invincibility of totalitarian systems':

'Of course, a Goliath has an interest in making himself and others believe that he is invincible. In fact, the totalitarian system is far weaker than it appears to be, because in the long run it cannot secure for itself the loyalty and the cooperation of the population. . . . We can, therefore, assume that the totalitarian system, together with a maximum of physical and military power, has a minimum of psychic power at its disposal. Its psychic weakness is the Achilles' heel of the totalitarian system.'

The importance which civilian defence theorists attribute to contact with the opponent must be seen in the light of what we have just discussed. Proposals include fraternisation with the occupant (see for instance Naess, 1958 and 1964b), increasing the exchange of persons and information with potential attackers (i.e., prior to attack) and many similar methods, all with the same purpose of building up confidence, breaking down stereotypes, etc. The fact that these approaches have been of limited utility in cases where *violent* means of resistance were used or contemplated is no convincing counter-argument because in the case of non-violent resistance, attack as well as repression are much more difficult for the occupier to justify or rationalise.

We have already dealt at length with the particular problems involved in combining 'positive' influencing techniques such as fraternisation with 'negative' techniques such as non-cooperation, problems which make it difficult to conceive of the first group as more than a relatively minor supplement to the second, but such problems and reservations do not arise with positive means applied *before* hostilities have begun.

b) Appealing to conscience

Here the aim is not to change the opponent's viewpoint but to appeal to his empathy or his basic humanitarianism. Strikes which hit *both* defender and occupier (the former often more heavily than the latter) are frequently seen as having this effect, and so are the self-immolations like those of Buddhist monks in Vietnam and of Jan Pallach in Czechoslovakia.

The latter are extreme examples of what Galtung calls the 'amplification of suffering'. The defender attempts to activate the conscience of the opponent by inflicting upon himself a higher level of suffering than that which directly results from the opponent's actions, but does so in such a way that the responsibility for the increased suffering is laid with the opponent. This is, of course, the idea in lying down in front of advancing tanks. Less dramatic examples of this technique are often quoted in the literature — for example the voluntary imprisonment of conscientious objectors in Britain during World War I which had a long term effect (legislation was eventually changed), but no apparent short term effect.

While there is little doubt that extreme measures of self-sacrifice often have a considerable impact on public opinion in the occupying country and abroad, there are numerous examples to show that they are not always effective in making the opponent desist from action. No examples from a long list of brutalities against unarmed and defenceless civilians need be mentioned to make this point.

There is to our knowledge only one laboratory experiment

which has been performed with the explicit aim of studying the psychological effect of non-violent techniques on the opponent, and its results were not too encouraging. In that study participants were made to bargain with a stooge about the way to share a pay-off between them and were given the further option of inflicting electric shocks upon the opponent to force him into submission. The stooge had been instructed to emphasise that he was morally committed to non-violence, that he would refuse to use shocks against the opponent and that he was determined to expose himself to shocks rather than accept an unfair deal. In a few participants these appeals produced the desired restraint, but for many others their resolve to dominate was increased by attributing trickery to the motives of the pacifist.

Altogether, participants confronted with a pacifist showed no greater tendency towards cooperative behaviour than did those who were not; nor could fear explain the results since it made no difference whether the pacifists were known to be 'disarmed' (no ability to inflict shocks) or not. The authors concluded that whereas pacifist appeals can dissuade some adversaries away from their original stance they fail to influence those who intend to dominate and may even encourage exploitation amongst those who do not have such intentions prior to interacting with the pacifist (Shure *et al.*, 1965).

Needless to say, there is scope for considerable scepticism about generalisations from such laboratory experiments to real life situations, and the degree of realism of this experiment, particularly as regards the participants' evaluation of the suffering inflicted upon others, is open to doubt. The most important critique is probably that which relates to the relevance of the experiment for civilian defence methods. In the experiment there were no external costs associated with brutal conduct, no-one except oneself to account to morally, and the participants found themselves in a situation in which they were mutually anonymous, had no past establishing their role patterns and no future in which the consequences of their acts would be judged. Thus the experiment presupposes — and that is undoubtedly a crude oversimplification — that the restrained behaviour which is expected of those who are confronted with a pacifist is due solely to his conscience in the narrow sense of individual psychology, whereas other factors like, for instance, a socially determined moral pressure are completely ignored.

Nevertheless, the strikingly negative result of these experiments at least provides a warning against an exaggeratedly simplistic view of what appeals to conscience can achieve in the direct relation between the occupying forces and the resistance, and without taking into account the full set of expectations and costs.

On the other hand appeals to conscience, the amplification of suffering and similar techniques may have effects other than those most emphasised by authors on non-violence. Even if they were not to cause much disaffection or mutiny they may nevertheless enhance the constraints imposed by the military professional ethics of the occupying troops regarding the use of force against unarmed civilians and thus, for instance, inhibit repression against non-cooperation. These constraints may well be quite powerful. As Liddell Hart (1967) points out the Germans often had considerable difficulty in knowing how to respond to non-violent resistance:

'The German generals, by and large were handicapped by the relatively humane tradition in which they had been brought up. They found it difficult to be as ruthless as military logic and military theory tended to demand.'

c) Splitting the Home Front

In the literature on civilian defence less attention has been paid to the possibility of creating dissent and opposition in the home country of the opponent, perhaps because this is more dependent on factors which are to a large extent outside the control of the resistance.

The invasion itself may exacerbate political divisions within the invader's home country. The immediate and spontaneous political reaction in Britain to British participation in the invasion of Suez in 1956 is a clear example of this. The resistance might in some cases be able to influence the situation by supplying information directly (the information offices abroad of the various national liberation movements serve this purpose). Propaganda aimed at the occupying forces achieves the same thing indirectly, but its effectiveness depends to a large extent on the ability to reach groups higher up in society than those from which rank-and-file troops are normally drawn, and the views of which do not spread very much to the remainder of the population.

The extent to which the defenders can exploit or create such opposition would depend on having a good knowledge of existing political divisions in the invader's home country and, preferably, prior contacts and continued communication with political groups there.

A good example of the effect of the resistance on the home front of the occupier is provided by the Franco-Belgian invasion of the Ruhr and the non-violent resistance of the Germans. The Belgian people openly condemned their government's adventure (Sternstein, 1967) and as Grimm wrote of the situation in France:

Opinions were changing. The economic consequences of the Ruhr occupation showed themselves everywhere. A nation like the French is unable to endure moral isolation for any length of time. The occupation had repercussions which no one had expected. Thousands of Frenchmen who went to the Ruhr as soldiers and civilians became *advocats des boches* intercessors on behalf of the Germans. For the first time they saw the Germans as they really are. They met an industrious people living in neat houses, people who were so very different from what war propaganda had led them to believe. There were even many high-ranking officers who had soon to be replaced as unsuitable because of their friendly attitude towards the Germans . . . In the elections of May 1924 the French themselves decided against the [hitherto ruling party coalition, the] Bloc National. (1930)

Another possibility is to provoke opposition within the occupying power's home country by making the costs inflicted by the defence intolerable ('costs' being taken here in its widest sense). Actual attrition of the occupying power is well-known, from guerrilla warfare, but is not so easy to visualise for a civilian defence. The protracted non-cooperation of the occupied population could conceivably lead to attrition, but the costs to the defendants would be very high in this case.

d) Mobilisation of International Support

Any realistic assessment of possible policies aimed at mobilising international support is of course utterly impossible without a very explicit scenario describing, not only the form of the occupation and of the resistance, but also the international context within which both take place. Even more than previously, the need for considering the total strategic and historical situation is inescapable in this case.

Undoubtedly the most important type of international pressure, particularly if one is dealing with the isolated occupation of a small West-European country would be the effect this would have on the other European countries. It would presumably make them gang together in common opposition to the occupant and increase their general military efforts so that, altogether, the position of the aggressing country would become worse, not better, as a result of the occupation. This, however, has more to do with the problem of deterrence, and is, therefore, dealt with in greater detail in a later chapter.

It would of course be naive to assume off-hand that support for a resistance movement or pressure against the occupant is necessarily motivated by support for the *aims* of the resistance movement. Strategies designed to mobilise external support would, therefore, seek to exploit not only the sympathies but also the self-interests of other nations or of powerful groups within other nations.

It is not suggested here that any of the possible consequences of occupation which would be effective in undermining the opponent's strength will necessarily materialise, nor that if they do they will have any great effect. On the other hand, an awareness that such effects may materialise could enable the civilian defence organisation to manipulate the situation more effectively than they already do.

CHAPTER III

Organisational Problems

In the literature a great deal of attention has been paid to particular types of organisation which may or may not be suitable for civilian defence. The picture which emerges is somewhat confused — a great deal of time is spent discussing such specific technical problems as delivery of milk or the growing of food in backyards, and little on the more basic issues involved.

The problems to be dealt with here are those relating to the organisation of society and the possibility of redressing those aspects which most contribute to the vulnerability of the society as well as the organisational forms which may be given to the civilian defence apparatus under occupation, particularly in so far as leadership and coordination are concerned and the question of whether the leadership should be centralised or not and whether it should be open, underground or in exile.

It is clear that in different types of society different organisational forms will be required. What is appropriate for an undeveloped country with a largely self-sufficient peasantry, a low degree of urbanisation, and poor transport and communication facilities, may not be suitable for a highly industrialised Western European nation.

1. THE VULNERABILITY OF SOCIETY

In much of the work on the preparations for an occupation defence, in particular with Carter (1964) and Galtung (1967), the concern has been with the reduction of the vulnerability of the civilian population to measures of mass repression from the opponent. Concern with the possibility of blockades, policies of starvation and with the possible consequences of dependence of an urban population on water, fuel and power supplies have led to proposals for stockpiling, de-centralisation to increase self-sufficiency, production of food concentrates etc.

There are several reasons, however, why the use of those repressive methods which, in principle, it would be possible to find a protection against (for example starvation of the population), do not seem particularly likely. First, it is difficult to imagine any strategic gain which might accrue to an occupying power which could offset the heavy costs (to the occupying power) in the form of protest and opposition abroad and declining political support at home which would arise if such extreme methods were implemented. Second, there would be less politically costly ways of achieving the same ends, for instance the selective use of terror against particular persons or groups to split the resistance. Third, the destruction of the economy of the occupied country would also greatly inconvenience the occupying forces. Last, but not least, such massive repression would either make the population give up non-violence and take up whatever arms are available, which cannot be in the interest of the occupying power, or else the population would presumably give in on the grounds that nothing can be gained from a continuation of the struggle. In the face of a policy of genocide, non-violent defence is virtually useless, and there is little else to do than hope for assistance from abroad. Scepticism is therefore justified regarding the usefulness of taking on the huge costs in peace time which would be involved in a de-centralisation of the economic and political systems as radical as Carter and Galtung imply.

De-centralisation of the economic system has also been advocated on other grounds. Some writers suggest a de-centralisation of the economy which would also make it less vulnerable to attempts at control, exploitation, tax collection etc. Carter mentions the small-factory system of southern Italy as an example. However, the examples of de-centralised economic systems given all typify underdeveloped economies and declining industries. De-centralisation of the economy to this level would without doubt cause a drastic decline in living standards and welfare services and would mean the transformation of the country into a warfare state, even in peace time.

The fact that countries become increasingly dependent on external trade and therefore vulnerable to blockade has led to similar suggestions for making each country more fully self-sufficient. Without denying that something might be achieved in this way it is nevertheless clear that one would soon encounter the same problem of a decline in welfare if such a policy were pursued. This is particularly so for countries with a very large foreign trade and for those countries which would have great difficulties in finding substitutes for indispensable imports such as foodstuffs or fuel. Besides it is to be noted that from the point of view of defence the international division of labour is not the only liability. The independence of Switzerland is to some extent safeguarded by the importance of the Alp tunnels for that country's neighbours. For other countries like South Africa and the oil producing countries of the Middle East their economic importance for the West, also provides some degree of protection for their regimes and political systems.

This is not to deny that certain limited measures might be useful in allowing the resistance movement a greater freedom of manoeuvre by reducing the cost of certain forms of non-cooperation. Similarly, this may serve to increase the feeling of security in the population, thus increasing the strength of the resistance, or to protect against the economic disruptions which the occupation can hardly fail to cause. The economic losses incurred through strikes and delivery stoppages will hit both the resistance and the occupant, but where the resistance takes the initiative it can try to keep the losses to the population at a minimum, and those of the occupying power at a maximum. Limited preventive stockpiling may, therefore, be of some utility. On the other hand, where it is the occupying power who takes the initiative his aim will be the opposite and it will always be possible to get around any preventive measures the population might have taken.

Another aspect of a highly industrialised system with an advanced technology which distinguishes it from less developed societies seems to be that in the first case it is more difficult or downright impossible to make the economy work efficiently using the cruder forms of coercion. Advanced industrial production requires a minimum of cooperation and even initiative on behalf of the workers. This affords some protection against the cruder forms of repression in those situations where the occupying power wishes to keep the economy going, while at the same time creating ideal conditions for Schweikism and go-slow tactics against which the occupying power can do very little.

It seems that one can summarise by saying that large scale measures to decentralise the economy and increase the ability of individual sectors to perform independently are excluded both because of the immense cost it would entail, and because even so it would be of little use. More limited measures might, on the other hand, provide the defence with greater flexibility in tactics. Moreover, and in contrast to what most authors seem to believe, the development from a self-sufficient peasant economy to a modern industrial state is not an unmitigated evil from the point of view of the defensive capability. At any rate the basic features of the economy and of the social structure in general must be treated as given in developing a defence system, since otherwise one is trying to defend something entirely different.

2. COORDINATION OF THE RESISTANCE

The increasing tendency towards interdependence and centralisation in modern industrial societies also means that the major public and private institutions are increasingly characterised by bureaucratic organisational structures with hierarchic chains of command. A major consequence of this is that, increasingly, only the incumbents of the top positions in the various institutions are in a position to be able to plan and coordinate policy. The lower the level in the hierarchy the less the understanding of the wider implications of the tasks performed. Incumbents of the lowest positions increasingly become functionaries with neither the knowledge nor the ability to influence overall policy.

In going through the arguments in the literature one is struck by the fact that the problem of coordination between groups and the problem of overall political and strategic control have been almost completely ignored in the discussion of decentralisation, in spite of the fact that the latter, undoubtedly, must make these problems much larger.

Where the strategy merely consists of a few simple directives like 'total non-cooperation' or 'work on without collaboration' then the problems of strategic planning and of organisation tend to disappear. 'Working on without collaboration' consists in obeying orders from legal but not from illegal authorities so that the resistance organisations must coincide with the major social institutions (public administration, private companies, etc.). The need for a strategic overview disappears, of course, when, in Ebert's words, every man becomes 'his own general'. However, such a 'strategy' can backfire (see below on the Ruhrkampf) and, furthermore, it may not be so simple for those in lower positions in the hierarchies to determine whether the instructions they receive were issued by the legal authorities or by collaborators.

If, on the other hand, the policy is to make use of the whole spectrum of methods it will hardly be possible to avoid some measure of strategic steering. This raises the problem of embodying the resistance organisation in the bureaucratic structures of the major institutions of the society, because these are so devised that people at the lower levels depend on those at the top, while the latter are both very visible and very vulnerable in an occupation. This is an important reason explaining why a majority of civilian defence writers have favoured a more decentralised organisation both for society as a whole, and for the resistance organisation. These writers have further claimed that decentralisation avoids bureaucratic delays so that the organisation can respond quickly and flexibly to changing situations without the inertial element which often characterises bureaucratic systems, while closer contact with the base of the organisation should lead to a wider outlook for those at the bottom, and more informed leadership at the top.

Sharp (1969) envisages that the 'free institutions' of society (voluntary and professional organisations, the press etc.), which are both collectively organised and semi-autonomous in relation to the state, could serve as the basic units of a resistance organisation. Sharp (and others) here draws on the experience of the Norwegian resistance (in particular the resistance of the teachers' organisations against the Quisling regime). Since the ostensible functions of many of the so-called 'free institutions' — in particular unions and the various professional associations — is the furtherance of the interests of their members, and since this gives them a certain experience in conflict with the state, business interests, etc. and a structure adapted to conflicts with external groups, they could perhaps play an important role if the top levels of business, administration and government had been taken over either by the occupying power or by collaborators. Historical precedents, including those considered later in this work, support this assumption. In other words these groups could, according to

59

Sharp, act as the centre of gravity for resistance in other methods, like that envisaged by Ebert (which relies primarily on resistance at the top of society) were to fail.

The role played by the radio in the Czechoslovak resistance in 1968 suggest a possible solution − at least in the short term − to the problem of reliable and fast communication and coordination. While instructions from the Party leadership were relayed to the public, it fell on the radio station staff to select and broadcast from the mass of incoming information on events throughout the country that which was relevant. Resistance tactics which had evolved in one part of the country were made known to the rest of the population in a matter of hours, and all forms of warnings and recommendations could be issued instantaneously. The potential that the use of radio networks in resistance offers, of course goes further than the successes achieved in Czechoslovakia, but that example unequivocally demonstrates how one may by-pass hierarchic command structures − with all that these imply in delay, information corruption and inefficiency − without losing a strategic overview and the potential for tight strategic and tactical control. Broadcasting to the whole nation with feedback coming in constantly through telephone link-ups means that, potentially, the whole population becomes one vast 'organisation' with a maximally informed leadership, a minimum number of communication links between top and bottom, and as much information at the base as is deemed necessary.

The lifespan of this kind of resistance organisation is of course determined by the ability of the underground radio networks to survive. While it seems unlikely that an occupying power will in the future repeat the mistakes the occupying powers made in Czechoslovakia there seems no *a priori* reason why with adequate research and planning one should not be able to establish a far better and less vulnerable system than the improvised set-up with which the Czechoslovaks had so much initial success.

As an extreme opposite to this form of organisation we may mention the 'cell' system which the Communists adopted in the occupied countries in the last war and which the FLN guerrillas used in Algeria. The system consists of a branching hierarchy of 'cells' at various levels with no connection between cells at the same level, and each of them having a dozen members or less. The lack of horizontal communication between cells and the fact that only one member of each cell needs to communicate upwards makes it almost impossible to trace the organisation, starting from one of its members, and equally impossible to paralyse it by cutting a limited number of communication links, despite the fact that it is hierarchically structured. No member is able to give away more than a handful of others. The system is not incompatible with a large degree of autonomy for each geographical region or for each sector in the economy, provided it was set up with this in mind. While this form of organisation has obvious drawbacks, it was developed and found suitable under conditions which placed a high premium on survival. It is probably the most appropriate system for a protracted underground resistance and to maintain continuity until conditions improve and more open forms of resistance can be used as happened in Europe in the last stages of the war.

3. THE LEADERSHIP: OPEN, UNDERGROUND AND IN EXILE

Together with the preference for a decentralised and more 'democratic' organisation which is found in the literature, and very much linked to it, there is a preference for a leadership which remains in the country, at its post for as long as possible, which participates openly in the resistance and which thereby serves as a model for the rest of the resistance movement. In this case too, the conclusion seems to be based in part on ideological preferences in addition to those arguments of a more pragmatic kind which are presented.

In fact, the question of openness versus secrecy of the resistance is much broader than that which we are suggesting here, because, ultimately, the same question arises when it comes to planning the various actions and the course of the struggle. For Gandhi the intentional use of untruthfulness is irreconcilable with the ultimate aim of full self-realisation (Naess, 1958) and in one form or another this conception pervades much of the whole literature. As noted in the introduction, such considerations do, however, fall outside the more limited and 'pragmatic' perspective we have chosen, and we shall therefore limit ourselves to considering under which circumstances open resistance and open leadership would be the most effective from the point of view of liberating the country.

Sharp (1971) lists a number of arguments against secrecy in general and for open leadership in particular. Other writers like Carter (1964) and Ebert (1967) have put forward similar arguments. Secrecy, says Sharp, is both rooted in and contributes to fear, while the courageousness of an open leadership, by providing an example to the resistance, helps to dispel fear. While openness increases the chances that the leaders will be arrested, imprisoned or otherwise repressed, this is not necessarily a bad thing in Sharp's view, since a willingness to face repression provides both example and encouragement to others, while the act of repression used against a popular leader may increase the antipathy towards the occupier and thus support for the resistance. The advantages of decentralisation are again stressed since this both reduces the dependence on leaders and the necessity for secrecy. The 'security consciousness' which is a prerequisite for a secret organisation reduces the number of those involved in the policy making process and can result in poor planning as a consequence of insufficient or corrupt information. Underground organisations, Carter adds, are also seen as breeding suspicion and distrust and as involving, for this reason, a risk of para-military take-over, of political and personal enemies being eliminated, etc. Finally, the restriction of the number of people participating in decisions is seen as undemocratic and thus likely to reduce the commitment of those who are excluded.

The impression gained is that many of these arguments are coloured by the fact that openness is advocated for its own sake, rather than as an instrument to build an effective resistance movement. Thus the advantages from repression being used against leaders should be set against the potential drawbacks. First, repression may deter others from taking over the leadership. Secondly, imprisoned leaders can only play a purely symbolic role whereas in an underground resistance they have little symbolic value but can serve instrumentally to plan the resistance. Moreover, an open leadership can be subjected to all kinds of pressures by the occupying power, or by the population itself, since the latter might very well have a more short-term political perspective than the leaders. Lastly, it must be assumed than an open leadership will be unable to secure correct information on ongoing events if the occupant tries to prevent it. The leaders might therefore be compelled to make decisions on a basis of false intelligence, carefully constructed by the occupant. It is also clear that many of the methods which have been proposed are of necessity (sabotage) or even by definition ('underground', press and radio) of a clandestine nature. In addition secrecy in planning is a necessity if the surprise element is to be maintained. All this suggests that an underground leadership has an important role to play right from the start and that there may well come a time when all forms of open resistance become impossible and where, instead, one must rely on methods which are themselves 'secret': Schweik-methods, go-slows, etc.

This brings us to another dilemma within the civilian defence literature, namely whether the government should remain within the occupied country or should go into exile.

The arguments one finds against a leadership in exile are similar to those for an open resistance leadership. It is assumed that if those who have a constitutional role as symbols of legitimacy (e.g. the King or the President) stand up against the occupier, this example will strengthen the resolve of the people and constrain the actions of the occupying power because other, more cooperative leaders cannot simply be put in their place. This argument, however, presupposes that the leaders do in fact take part in the resistance, whereas historical precedents indicate accommodation as the most typical response of the leadership.

The Head of State has an important role being alone constitutionally empowered to nominate the government and the government has a similar legitimising function in regard to the central administration. At least in the short run, their importance in these respects is not dependent on whether they go into exile. The advances by the Greek colonels to the King, both before and during his exile, demonstrate the importance which formal recognition by the Head of State entails for a regime which attempts to establish itself and to achieve a modicum of legitimacy.

The act of going into exile both removes the most visible and vulnerable leaders from pressure from the occupying power and implies a complete rejection of accommodation or submission. It thus makes it difficult for the occupant to establish a government which has the appearance of legitimacy and which claims to represent the resistance and the people. The occupying power would be free to establish a collaborationist government of the Quisling type, but this would not have the benefit of legitimacy and thus resistance against it could be made completely unequivocal. If communication permits, one might have both an exile government and an underground deputy government in the country itself. Ebert (1967) proposes a rotation whereby only some of the leaders are in exile at any time.

Government or other national figures vested with legitimacy and prestige who remain abroad though in close contact with the leadership in the occupied country could also have a central role in all attempts to mobilise sections of world opinion against the occupying power.

4. SUMMARY: THE NEED FOR FLEXIBILITY

It is almost impossible to discuss organisational requirements for civilian defence in the abstract without some knowledge of the objectives of the opponent (economic exploitation, ideological crusade, invasion with a wider strategic aim, etc.) and of the international political context in which the invasion takes place. It seems evident, however, that corresponding to different strategic situations, one will have to think of different levels of organisation, just as one finds in guerrilla warfare. Indeed it seems to us that many of the arguments about openness and secrecy, centralisation and decentralisation etc. miss the point in that they seek to establish the advantages and drawbacks of particular organisational forms in some absolute sense, when in fact their effectiveness varies as the context changes.

In guerrilla warfare the necessity for different organisational forms is clearly recognised. Where the guerrillas are weak and a strategy of attrition of the enemy is employed, organisation is relatively decentralised and of an underground character. Individual guerrilla units are allowed considerable tactical autonomy although the Party leadership retains the overall strategic control. As the opponent weakens and the guerrillas gain in strength the units link up, resistance becomes more open and the political leadership exercises tactical as well as strategic control. Flexibility of response is seen as crucial and the necessity to shift back and forth between the different levels by de-escalation or escalation as the situation demands, is constantly emphasised without de-escalation being in any way tainted with the odium of defeatism. This is undoubtedly a lesson which may be most profitably applied to civilian defence organisational planning.

In fact one gets the impression that those who have considered civilian defence hardly attribute any importance to the need for a common strategy. Sharp has a conception of several stages in a confrontation which require different forms of non-cooperation, but he does not seem to have any clear idea of how the decision to pass from one stage to the next is to be reached. In the historical cases most quoted in the literature (for instance the Ruhrkampf and Czechoslovakia) there was, despite the large measure of improvisation, nevertheless some form of strategic guidance, and this is even more so with other types of non-violent campaigns such as Gandhi's struggle for the independence of India and the Civil Rights movement in the United States. Only in a few cases of brief and unplanned action (as, for instance the civilian insurrections in San Salvador in 1944, in Guatemala in 1945 and in Chile in 1961; see Lakey, 1969) does one find the relatively spontaneous and entirely 'democratic' civilian action which many advocates of civilian defence seem to have in mind.

We shall deal with this at greater length in the next chapter, but it seems to us that it is impossible to envisage a non-violent defence against occupation which merely takes the form of a spontaneous and improvised insurrection. Whether there is any need for peace-time preparations may be debated, but once occupation has taken place there is undoubtedly a need for a general strategic plan for the entire struggle and for people who can draw it up and implement it. An occupying power would be able to adapt to any policy which was completely settled in advance, say, the rule of 'working on without collaboration'.

Whether the resistance takes an open or underground form will depend on the stage of the struggle, the strength of the opponent, his willingness to use heavy repression, and its effectiveness if used. An open resistance coordinated through a clandestine radio network like that in Czechoslovakia can only last as long as the underground radio stations survive. On the other hand, open resistance of the type advocated by Ebert can last as long as repression remains bearable because, as already noted, such strategies as 'work on without collaboration' do not in themselves presuppose any organisational form or political or strategic perspective. If, however, repressive counter-strategies against general open resistance are effective then retrenchment to more diffuse resistance tactics is indicated — perhaps through the 'free institutions' as Sharp and others have suggested. At this stage the importance of localised resistance organisations having some considerable autonomy becomes obvious — though again it must be emphasised that these organisations should be tied into the underground resistance infrastructure if the overall resistance effort is to retain some measure of coordination. Finally, there might well be periods when any form of open resistance comes to be seen as too dangerous so that attrition tactics (like Schweikism and 'go-slow') which can be most easily maintained because they are almost impossible to detect must become the main focus of the resistance.

In other words the general pattern would appear to be a move from open to underground and from centralised and inter-dependent to centralised but more autonomous organisational forms and methods if the opponent's control over the situation increases. The key to effectiveness would seem to lie in eschewing rigid formulae and being prepared to shift from one strategic level to another and back again as the situation demands.

As regards the position of the leadership it seems useful to distinguish between its three functions. First, there is the con-stitutional role as a source of legitimacy, with all the possibilities this implies for preventing a collaborationist government from taking over, establishing diplomatic relations with other countries, etc. It seems essential to protect this role as far as possible from the occupying power's attempts to control it, and it is therefore reasonable to think of exile in this case. As noted, there is also an important task in seeking support abroad, and because of the symbolism and prestige associated with his position, the Head of State is particularly suited for that task.

Another function for the leadership is the legislative and executive one and the day-to-day strategic and tactical steering of the resistance. For this it is of course necessary to be on the spot, and, equally, it is necessary that those who fulfil this role are protected from the opponent's attempts at coercion and control of information. This part of the leadership must therefore necessarily go into hiding if it is to serve any useful purpose apart from maintaining the morale of the population.

This last and purely symbolic role should, however, not be underestimated. On the other hand it seems that it can be fulfilled equally well, or even better sometimes, by other persons instead of the political and administrative leaders. The important point is simply that they be well-known and respected public figures, that they appear openly, and that they are not irreplaceable because they must necessarily be in a vulnerable position, making it easy for the occupant to remove them, imprison them, or render them harmless in other ways. Finally, it is essential that such persons should not be given any formal power of decision making because the occupant can subject them to pressure. An illustration of this symbolic leadership is the role played in the Czechoslovak resistance by the sports hero Zatopek.

At any rate the assumption that the leadership should simply come forward and act as a model of courageous behaviour should not be taken for granted. As has become clear in Czechoslovakia, the need for unity in the resistance is so dominant a concern that the strength of the resistance is determined, not by the strongest, but by the weakest links of the chain, and the weakest link could well turn out to be the leaders (see below on the undermining of the Czechoslovak resistance).

CHAPTER IV

The Analogy with Guerrilla Warfare

The many and obvious points of similarity between civilian defence and guerrilla warfare have not attracted much attention so far. This is undoubtedly related to the lack of theoretical analysis, which is a general characteristic of recent works on civilian defence. Galtung, in an article in *Pax* (1965b), calls attention to the analogy and stresses of certain of its components but without going much into depth. Bondurant (1962) considers the opposite problem, how to *combat* guerrillas with non-violent means. Other writers (Roberts, 1967b; Gwynne-Jones, 1967; and, to a lesser extent Liddell Hart, 1967) have also tended to emphasize the problem of combating guerrillas rather than the possibility of learning from their methods.

Instead of this analogy another one is emphasised. There is an almost universal tendency to discuss non-violent defence — i.e. the use of non-violent methods in national defence — together with examples of non-violent campaigns such as the Civil Rights movement in the United States and the nuclear disarmament campaigns of the early 'sixties. Evidently, the validity of such an analogy between campaigns which have nothing in common except their use of similar 'weapons' (tactics) is limited, at best, to the tactical level, that is to the ways of using these 'weapons' in a direct confrontation. Instances of non-violence being used in national defence, i.e. against foreign occupation, are few (two such instances are discussed in some detail in Chapter VI) and the tendency to use only non-violent campaigns as illustrations and guides to thinking has led to an almost complete neglect of the strategic aspects of a struggle against foreign domination as contrasted with its tactical moments.

68

THE ANALOGY WITH GUERRILLA WARFARE

Compared with non-violent occupation defence, guerrilla warfare is a fairly frequent phenomenon, and there are grounds for believing that a study of guerrilla campaigns — of those which never materialised, those which failed, and those which succeeded alike — could improve substantially our understanding of some of the sociological, psychological, political and strategic factors which would be involved in protracted resistance and attrition strategies, whether violent or not. The parallels that can be drawn between this form of warfare and civilian defence seem to us to be much more important and to dig much deeper than the parallels between either of these and 'conventional' military defence.

It would lead us too far from the main theme of this work to conduct anything like a thorough analysis of the different aspects of guerrilla warfare and to draw the relevant conclusions for civilian defence. We shall therefore merely call attention to some of the important aspects of the analogy which directly clarify the conditions of civilian defence. It needs saying, however, that guerrilla warfare, of course, is no uniform phenomenon and that it is a crude simplification to treat it as a single, well defined and homogeneous category as we do below.

1. FUNCTIONS OF VIOLENCE IN GUERRILLA WARFARE

An obvious *difference* between guerrilla warfare and civilian defence lies, of course, in the espousal of violence in the former and its rejection in the latter. It might also be thought that the use of violence provides an important parallel between military and guerrilla strategies. The latter is perhaps only true in a rather superficial sense. In conventional military theory violence aims at physical destruction with a view, ultimately, to punish the enemy (in deterrence strategy) or to demoralise him (in the actual conduct of war). Compared with guerrilla theories of the functions of violence these are very crude conceptions of its possible uses.

Guerrilla theorists have stressed the positive effects of violence on those who employ it, the positive effects of being subjected to violence, as well as the direct and indirect consequences of the use of violence on the opponent. The parallel with civilian defence lies in the fact that the beneficient effects of non-violence claimed by its proponents are quite similar to those which guerrilla theorists claim for violence.

a) Effect of Committing Violence

Involvement in violent action is seen by the overwhelming majority of guerrilla strategists as having the function of rooting out habits of submission, deference and fearfulness which are associated with lifelong oppression. Violence is said to 'create new men' (Mao, 1968; Giap, 1962; Guevara, 1961; Debray, 1967; Fanon, 1968).

Exactly the same positive effect is claimed to result from participation in non-violent action (Sharp, 1965; Farmer, 1965; Luther King, 1964; Nehru, 1946; and others). Since the effects claimed do in fact occur in actual conflict situations it may be assumed that they are the manifestations of a process common to both violent and non-violent action against an opponent. Presumably these psychological changes result from a new and stronger identification with one's group, which is itself a consequence of the conflict (Coser, 1956) and are quite unrelated to the specific means used in waging struggle, whether violent or not.

b) Effect of being Subjected to Violence

This is the reverse side of the coin. As will be argued in a subsequent chapter on the effects of repression, the use of violence *against* a group may increase its internal cohesion (Coser, 1956) and widen support for the aims of the group. Both guerrilla theorists and civilian defence writers show an awareness of this phenomenon which Gregg (1960) calls 'moral jiu jitsu' to characterise the fact that the use of violence rebounds to the disadvantage of those who employ it. In both cases methods have been designed and applied to exploit this effect.

c) Violence as a Means of Inflicting Losses

The objective of the guerrilla strategist is not so much to reduce the military capability of the opponent (in terms of combatants killed, equipment destroyed, etc.) but rather to force the opponent to over-extend geographically and temporally, thus raising his maintenance costs. In other words the objective is essentially political: to undermine the opponent's resolve to continue the struggle. This is achieved partly amongst the troops in the field, but, more importantly, on the home front. Again, this indirect strategy has obvious points of similarity with civilian defence while it is very uncharacteristic of conventional military strategy. Even though violence, used as a means of inflicting losses, only plays a secondary role in guerrilla warfare, it does, of course, occur, and to the extent this is so, a meaningful parallel can be drawn with conventional warfare.

d) Terrorism

In guerrilla strategy selective terrorism serves as a punishment or a warning against collaboration. In civilian defence collaboration is punished by ostracism, social boycott or the like. Terrorism is, however, a more flexible means than those available to a civilian resistance leadership since it can operate even where the moral community which forms the basis of social sanctions is absent. Despite relatively extensive use in Vietnam, guerrilla strategists have nevertheless generally been hesitant in their attitude towards terrorism for the obvious reason that, carried too far, it can undermine the popular support upon which the guerrillas depend. Positive sanctions — rewards — such as agrarian reform have been stressed as being preferable to punitive actions such as terrorism.

e) The Final Strategic Offensive

In the theories of both Giap and Mao the final stage in a guerrilla war is the move to 'mobile warfare' by gathering the guerrillas into larger units and using them to confront the weakened and demoralised opponent on his own conventional military terms. Throughout his works Mao repeatedly stresses the point that while guerrilla warfare can prevent defeat it can never win victory on its own.

Mobile warfare appears to serve two aims: First, the regroupment of the troops serves to create a revolutionary army which is seen as an indispensable instrument in establishing the post-war revolutionary society. Contrary to a widespread misconception the armed struggle in Mao's theory is not the revolution itself, only its prerequisite. The seizure of power and the political mobilisation created in the struggle only provide the basis for the political role of the revolutionary army. This particular function has no equivalent in civilian defence because the aim of the latter is supposed to be the re-establishment of the *status quo ante.*

The second aim of the final offensive is, of course, to force the enemy to capitulate or to withdraw. But it is not clear that this is an absolutely necessary stage if the aim is simply to force a foreign power to withdraw after a war of attrition (France from Indo-China and Algeria, and the United States from Vietnam).

The question of the necessity of a final, more intense phase in a non-violent struggle has not had much attention so far. Nor are there any convincing precedents to go by. In the last phase of a war conventional and guerrilla warfare are no longer distinguishable, and it is not unlikely that a non-violent resistance movement would yield to the temptation of using violence at this point, where reprisals are unlikely and where a sharp rise in the direct costs to the occupying power might hasten his withdrawal.

2. SOCIAL DEFENCE AND TERRITORIAL DEFENCE

Galtung (1965b) distinguishes two orientations to defence which he calls 'social defence' and 'territorial defence'. The emphasis in the former is on the defence of social and political institutions, while in the latter the emphasis is on retaining control over territory and preventing penetration of the frontiers. Galtung holds that both guerrilla warfare and civilian defence are oriented towards social defence while conventional military thinking is rather oriented towards the territorial concept of defence. In offensive strategy the conventional military approach also emphasises territorial gain in contrast to offensive guerrilla strategy which consists in undermining the social and political institutions of the opponent either directly or indirectly.

It seems to us that caution is indicated when seeing, as Galtung does, the social or territorial character of the defence as a question of ends, of 'what is to be defended' — a way of discussing the problem which is very widespread among the proponents of civilian defence. The difference between the two concepts of defence seems rather to be related to the different tactical and strategic conditions under which they operate.

The guerrilla fighter and the civilian defender are both confronted with the same problem, to defend themselves against an opponent which has an overwhelming superiority in conventional military terms (weapons systems and logistics, i.e., supply systems in the broadest sense), and in either case they have no option but to refuse to meet the opponent on his chosen ground, to avoid him where he attacks, attack him where he is weakest, and altogether seek to tire him and wear down his forces. The strategic resources available to the resistance are mainly men, political will, time and sometimes space. Such resources, however, should not be under-estimated. They directly imply the main elements of the strategy: a war of attrition in which the opponent is allowed to occupy the country: reliance upon the population for protection, cover, logistic support, communication and supplies; the systematic use of tactical retreat; and the need for being continuously on the offensive politically.

In contrast to the guerrillas the occupation defence does not have the problem that it must win over the population to its side in the course of the struggle, but the importance of this difference is perhaps less than may appear. Even where public opposition to the occupation is unanimous there remains a considerable task in mobilising the resistance, in welding it into a powerful, politically conscious movement with a coherent strategy and an understanding of the tactical means available. Writers on civilian defence have tended to ignore these problems completely. In civilian defence as in guerrilla war, a comprehensive and continuous effort at political mobilisation is the necessary foundation for actions against the opponent.

While advocates of a military defence have laid the main emphasis on the continued existence of the State, on national sovereignty and territorial inviolability, the advocates of civilian defence have instead stressed the preservation of the life style and culture of the population and social institutions as the ultimate aims. Nevertheless it constantly transpires that civilian defence advocates after all espouse a territorial concept of defence, and this is particularly true of those who belong to the 'pragmatic' school. Mostly, it is explicitly stated that the final aim is the expulsion of enemy troops. The relatively lesser interest of these authors in territorial 'integrity' in part stems from the tactical and strategic conditions because those means which are available to the defence can only be used after invasion has taken place, and in part it reflects a certain real difference in value priorities because guerrilla war and civilian defence, in contradistinction to military defence, are *also* interested in social and cultural values. The latter interest can also in part be seen as a consequence of strategic and tactical needs because the active support of the population is so crucial to these forms of struggle.

When, as an example of social defence carried to the extreme, Galtung, in the article referred to above mentions the Jews in Diaspora — a nation without a territory, but with a life style of its own — then that example, perhaps, illustrates, — not the possibility of a social defence which is unrelated to territory or State, but rather its impossibility; what the Jews succeeded in 'defending' in Diaspora were more or less ritualistic cultural patterns and a very limited set of social institutions of a 'private' character. But even these cultural patterns and social institutions have no autonomous existence because all of the institutions of the larger society in turn affect the individuals' life styles and value orientations. As with the Jews who have had to adapt to conditions in each country separately, so a 'pure' social defence in Galtung's sense would in fact amount to a *cultural* defence in the narrow meaning of the term.

Apart from relatively minor differences in emphasis the idea that social and territorial defence are based on different value orientations seems to result from a confusion of means and ends. Neither war for the guerrillas, nor occupation for the advocates of civilian defence are representative of the life style and the social conditions which it is hoped to create or to preserve. The form of struggle chosen is, of course, merely a temporary lesser evil, not an ideal, and no inference can be drawn from it to the effect that there is a lack of concern for territory.

It is quite another thing, however, to ask what is to be meant by the word 'territory', for civilian defence writers have a clear tendency to downgrade the importance of uninhabited and economically unimportant parts of the territory. This, again, must be seen in the light of the difference between the strategies suited to military and to civilian defence, not as an independent value premise. A base area on an otherwise useless strip of land or an island in the Arctic Ocean has a strategic importance within a conventional military defence conception (at least the importance resulting from the opponent's not gaining access), while its value is rather limited for the guerrillas and virtually zero for non-violent defence. It is, no doubt, precisely the military importance of even those territorial outposts which from a civilian point of view are most useless which has made the 'national territory', its sanctity and 'integrity', such important national symbols.

If one is to discuss which are the 'values' which the defence system ought to be designed to defend, it is necessary, first, to distinguish those 'values' which are intrinsically important from those which merely derive from the strategic and tactical demands of existing military defence systems and which, in the last analysis, are therefore means, not ends. 'Territorial integrity' is undoubtedly of this kind if taken in its uncompromising meaning. It is therefore no substantial critique of civilian defence that there are certain peripheral areas it cannot defend.

Different approaches to defence also give rise to conflicting conceptions of what constitutes victory and defeat. In both conventional military thinking and in international law these concepts are directly related to control of territory, while in both civilian defence and guerrilla warfare such formal criteria are rejected. Here too one can of course interpret the rejection of traditional conceptions of defeat intact, making a virtue out of strategic necessity, the necessity, being to give the forces of the opponent access to the territory in order to fight them more effectively. But it is also implied in the concept of a people's defence that formal criteria of the existence and sovereignty of the state do not play the same decisive role they do for a military defence since the latter is more directly the instrument of the state than of the people. Even where guerrillas or a non-violent resistance do concede a formal 'victory' to their opponents the changes they wish to implement may still be substantially achieved (the Ruhrkampf of 1923, discussed below, in some respects provides an illustration of this). In some types of internal conflicts, Bienen (1968) notes, the outcome is not substantially affected by who wins or loses in a conventional sense. In Algeria, independence — the goal of the insurgents — followed a conventional military victory for the French forces (Crozier, 1969).

3. UNEQUAL CONFRONTATION

The study of guerrilla warfare could provide important indications of what a confrontation would look like if it took place between two parties with so completely different means as those available to civilian defence and military attack. If non-violent actions are to serve any useful purpose in such a situation a strategic conception will be required which has little in common with those prevailing today, and even though it may differ in important respects from guerrilla warfare strategies, problems analagous to both require resolution. At any rate the same need would arise for finding other resources other than armament industries, troop strength and fire power.

If civilian defence were to be considered seriously as an alternative to military defence the main psychological barrier one would encounter would be precisely the belief, firmly held by most people, that the potential for physical destruction is a more effective means of influence than any other and that if it came to a test, manpower, the sophistication of weaponry and industrial potential would be decisive in the end.

The reasons for this belief are fairly obvious. Western strategic notions are pervaded by the idea of deterrence by potential destruction. This and the need to find a justification for the enormous intellectual and material resources invested in modern military establishments creates the psychological setting in which the over-simplified view can prevail that a potential for physical destruction can only be countered by a similar potential. Historical examples, from the easy victories over non-European peoples in the colonial period and from the 'industrial' wars, mainly the two world wars, might seem to confirm the pre-eminence of industrial power in war.

It is none the less clear that this view does not stand up to closer scrutiny *unless*, in fact, the conflict was defined from the outset as a question of mutual destruction of military forces, i.e. unless the parties willingly recognise defeat when their military forces are crushed.

The guerrilla wars of the past half century and particularly the two Indo-China wars have demonstrated unambiguously that the ability of a power with a vastly superior technology and industry to win over a weaker opponent cannot be taken for granted. In fact, the guerrilla strategists have succeeded in turning the asymmetry of the situation to their advantage by avoiding confrontation with the opponent in situations where his technical superiority can be used, and by conducting their offensive operations in other than military areas.

THE ANALOGY WITH GUERRILLA WARFARE

The fundamental assumption of guerrilla strategy is that the physical attrition of the opponent which a military system based on industrial potential seeks to achieve can be countered by a strategy which aims at the political attrition of the opponent and which bases itself on the political mobilisation of the population. ' . . . if the totality of the population can be made to resist surrender, this resistance can be turned into a war of attrition which will eventually and inevitably be victorious'. (Katzenbach, 1962).

Both guerrilla warfare and civilian defence advocates have laid great emphasis on the indirect and political consequences of the struggle. Basic to the writings of Mao Tse-Tung is the belief that nations with legislative bodies simply cannot take a war of attrition, either financially, or in the long run, psychologically. In a multiparty system, or confronted with other forms of political opposition, the very fact of committing oneself to a protracted war is politically so suicidal that it is impossible.

For the guerrillas the principal objective is to force the opponent to over-extend geographically or otherwise over-stretch his forces while conducting costly and pointless search and control operations. For Mao Tse-Tung, retreat is not only a tactical necessity at particular stages in the struggle, it is an *offensive* operation when viewed in a *strategic* perspective, for the more one can afford to hand over to the opponent, the more he will have to defend. Similarly, the willingness of the civilian defence to let the enemy troops occupy the country must be seen as part of an offensive strategy.

The Vietnam war provides an example of a war of attrition in which indirect and political costs may become decisive. Militarily neither side could gain a conventional victory, but in the United States the endless prolongation of the war and the accumulating maintenance costs with no apparent pay-off gave rise to doubts and dissent about the necessity and the utility of continuing it. As the years of struggle continued America's war in Vietnam became a political burden and possibly an economic one as well. Without denying that there was a moral component to the American domestic opposition to the war there is nevertheless little doubt that it was primarily the cost to the United States and not the cost to the Vietnamese which has been decisive. The growing moral outcry was more a symptom of the changing American mood than a cause of it.

The idea of avoiding the impact of the forces of the opponent is also found in the literature on non-violent defence. Liddell Hart (1967) emphasises that delaying tactics ("Schweikism" and 'go-slow') cannot be countered by force, that, indeed, there is really no answer to such methods. ' . . . it might well prove necessary to bring in one's own officials, military and civil, which would place an enormous strain on one's resources; and even that does not work very effectively.'

Liddell Hart goes on to recommend that the enemy be compelled to disperse his forces:

. . . the more concentrated anything is in the way of non-violent resistance, the less force is required. The more general and widespread it is, the more difficult it is to deal with. The more the occupying forces can be made to spread, the more complex their problems become. That, I would say, should be the guiding principle in planning civilian defence, and an attempt should be made to adopt strategies and methods which cause maximum strain and therefore overstretch. (*Ibid.*)

If civilian defence is to work against attacks using military means it is necessary to develop a strategic doctrine specifically designed for this purpose, just as it was a condition for the struggle of the Asiatic peasant societies against the Western industrial powers. In the writings on civilian defence one finds nothing except scattered hints on strategy and some of these have been dealt with elsewhere in this work. In addition to means for preventing the opponent from exploiting his conventional superiority it seems absolutely necessary to have offensive strategic means available. The most useful conception in this area is probably the idea of splitting and undermining the opponent — occupying troops and domestic population in the opponent's homeland alike — by exploiting the weak moral position he has put himself in as a consequence of having attacked in the first place. Of course, there is a long way to go from such a notion to a full-fledged offensive strategy, and an even greater distance to a strategy for the total confrontation. At this point the aim has simply been to stress the need for developing such strategies. Their form is discussed at some length in Chapter X.

For the smaller countries of Western Europe with large neighbours and with a hopeless military situation, such as, say,

Denmark, the development of a strategy to make use of the resources effectively available rather than one which assumes off-
hand that an invasion would necessarily have to be met at the
level of conventional military defence is all the more important,
whether one strives for a non-violent or for another form of defence. All strategy consists in avoiding the enemy where he is
strong and attacking him where he is weak. Looking at actual
defence efforts in countries like Denmark in this light makes them
seem so primitive that one comes to wonder whether at all the
task has been taken seriously. Most of all it calls to mind Mao
Tse-Tung's example from the Abyssinian war where the troops
come forward to fight on the enemy's terms and died with hon-
our, in glory — and in vain.

4. GUERRILLA WARFARE IN URBAN SOCIETIES

In comparing guerrilla warfare and civilian defence the aim has
been to show that the similarities between them are so important that a further study of guerrilla warfare might be rewarding
for the analysis of the strategic, political, psychological and
sociological aspects of civilian defence.

To pre-empt any misunderstanding it must be stressed that it is
only at a relatively abstract and general level that the analogy is
meaningful. This might appear more clearly after briefly surveying the reasons why guerrilla warfare must be considered unsuitable as national defence for a small industrialised country, even in
case there were no hesitations on ethical grounds against using
violence.

The idea of using some variant of guerrilla warfare as national
defence in industrialised countries has received some attention
from western writers (Kennan, 1958; Liddell Hart, 1960), but
only in those countries whose geography and history give some
reason to think that it might work (such as Switzerland, Finland
and Yugoslavia) has this been taken at all seriously. In these
cases what is involved is a partisan war or armed resistance in
mountain or forest areas which can be extremely effective but
which is hardly applicable to countries with a greater population
density and less suitable geographic conditions.

Among the principal authors on guerrilla war it is only
Guevara (1961) who considers guerrilla-like operations in cities,
and even he only visualises this as an **urban** insurrection which

can assist the forces in the countryside by paralysing industry and commerce. The rural guerrillas retain their leading role.

The environmental factor is one of the main determinants of the feasibility of a guerrilla campaign. At least three of its aspects have a bearing upon strategy:

First, the *geographical extent* of the area determines the degree to which the enemy can be forced to disperse his troops and sustain long, vulnerable lines of communication and supply. On this point the urban guerrilla is worse off, mainly because the opponent has no communication and supply problems and can regroup previously dispersed units at very short notice.

Another environmental factor is the ability to *hide*, either in the terrain or by mixing with the local population. This enables the guerrillas to gather substantial forces in one spot without attracting notice and disperse them again, immediately after having attacked. For such tactics urbanised areas seem to be at least as well suited as are those where guerrilla fighters are normally found.

The third, and, from our point of view, perhaps the most important factor is the degree of protection provided by the environment. On this point the urban guerrilla suffers a hopeless handicap. Individual guerrillas may disappear in the crowd but the population as a whole is extremely vulnerable. In places like Vietnam a gigantic war machine will generally be needed to make effective reprisals against the population. Even at a comparable level of destruction reprisals are likely to be less effective in bringing pressure to bear on the guerrillas because of low population density, the population's relative independence of external supplies and the lower rate of diffusion of information. On each of these counts the city dweller is less well off.

In a relatively small, densely populated and industrialised society it is therefore hard to see how guerrilla war in the usual meaning of the term could be carried out and particularly how it could be used for national defence. On the one hand it would be difficult to wage a war of atrrition against the occupant, and on the other the local population would be so vulnerable that the popular support for the guerrillas could be reversed relatively easily. Use of non-violent methods instead, would undoubtedly reduce the likelihood of reprisals against the population, but it is hard to see how attrition could be achieved, i.e. how to impose sufficient losses on the opponent. As noted elsewhere it is the *indirect* costs to the occupant (and the direct benefits) which the civilian defence is best able to affect.

Urban guerrillas have gained prominence in recent years with the growth of the Tupamaros movement in Uruguay. In this case, however, tactical and strategic conditions differ considerably from those which would apply during occupation. Because the enemy, the Government, is not external but internal, and because this enemy itself needs the support, or at least the passive acquiescence of the population it cannot, as an occupying power might have done, resort to extensive reprisals against the population as a whole in order to isolate and suppress the guerrilla movement. It is also the case that the opponent of the urban guerrillas, the Government, is in this case much more vulnerable than is an occupying force, and all its functions, not only its troops, are exposed to the counter-reprisals of the guerrillas. It would therefore be rash indeed to conclude from the initial successes of the Tupamaros movement that an occupation defence based on urban guerrilla warfare would have the same prospects of success.

CHAPTER V

The Ability to Withstand Repression

As noted by many critics, arguments for the efficacy of civilian defence stand and fall on the ability of the resistance as an organised whole and of the individuals of which it is composed to withstand repression or the threat of repression. This is not only one of the most important but also one of the least researched subjects in the area of civilian defence and, consequently, the remarks below are of a very tentative nature.

Most of the advocates of non-violence have argued their case in the abstract and have not considered particular strategic situations. The main argument has been that the occupier cannot secure effective control without the compliance of the occupied, and it is therefore claimed that a really determined resistance which defies all attempts at repression will ultimately succeed because the opponent can gain nothing from persevering.

This contains on the one hand the important and far from trivial sociological insight, first developed in the sixteenth century by Etienne de la Boétie in his book *De La Servitude Volontaire* (On Voluntary Serfdom), that all rule, including tyranny, depends on the willingness of men to obey. On the other hand it fails to draw the obvious conclusion from this and from the fact that tyrannical regimes have existed and do exist; that the will of men itself depends on social conditions. The rise of the Nazi party in Germany in the wake of the depressions from 1918 to 1924 and again from 1929 onwards, and its almost complete withering in the intermediate period is, perhaps, the best illustration of this. In treating the opinions of men as *a priori* factors instead of relating them to the prevailing socio-economic conditions the literature on non-violence and civilian defence once more reveals its idealistic foundation (in the philosophical sense).

The problem of the ability of the resistance to persevere therefore involves at least three separate issues: first, the ability of individuals to stick to their original views and withstand intimidation by the threat of use and the actual use of force; second, the ability of the occupying power to so manipulate the social and economic conditions of the occupied country that various groups become pitted against one another and that loyalties change to the advantage of the occupying power, and, finally, the part technical, part sociological question of the occupying power's ability to prevent the individual will to resist from crystallising into coordinated group action, for without coordination the will to resist loses almost all effectiveness and is unlikely to even manifest itself on any large scale for reasons set out in the above discussion of the functions of symbolic actions.

Important though all of them are, we shall be concerned in this chapter with the first of these factors only, the effect of intimidation. To consider the other two factors in the abstract seems almost impossible and is not attempted here, but the analysis of some historical cases in later chapters should provide some preliminary indications of the problems they give rise to. An analysis of the way in which the Greek putsch-colonels have hitherto been able to prevent all coordinated resistance would shed considerable light on the third factor, but this is not attempted here.

We may initially make a broad and necessarily vague distinction is made here between 'limited' repression and 'massive' repression. The former refers to such measures as the imposition of censorship and of martial law, the prohibition of meetings etc., and also to what one might call 'exemplary' or 'random' violence, violence which seeks to persuade the population to comply out of an assessment of likely costs and benefits. By massive repression on the other hand, we mean violence which is aimed at forcing compliance by actually making the costs of resistance very high. Examples include the strategic bombing of German cities during the last war, the Soviet response to the Hungarian uprising in 1956, and the American bombing raids in the 'free strike zones' of South Vietnam.

WAR WITHOUT WEAPONS
1. THE EFFECT OF LIMITED REPRESSION

As a general rule it seems to be the case that low levels of repression act to increase support for the resistance and to increase the morale of those who resist. Actually, leaders of resistance movements sometimes seek repression (or what is perceived of as repression) in order to increase support for their movement. This technique, whether consciously used or simply occurring naturally has been called 'political jiu jitsu' (Sharp, 1965; Gregg, 1960), to emphasize the paradox that repression by the more powerful group increases the relative power of the weaker groups. It does so in three ways; first, by increasing the internal solidarity of the resistance; second, by increasing external support for it; and, third, by increasing dissent within the enemy ranks (provided counter-reprisals by the resistance do not occur).

An example to illustrate what is meant is provided by the increased public support for the Civil Rights marchers following the brutal repression by the police in the American South in the early 1960's. Another example is provided by the student activist groups, some of which have shown acute awareness of the utility of provoking repression to increase unity among the students. Thus the Mexican students deliberately provoked the police until one of them was killed, thus providing a martyr for the cause.

It may be noted in this connection that 'repression' is a value-laden term and that it is precisely in those cases where this word is seen as appropriate to describe what might otherwise appear as 'restoring law and order' that repression works to the advantage of the resistance. It is not the act itself but the context in which it is seen that matters.

For this mechanism to work it is of course essential that there be a reserve of potential support either in the form of previously uncommitted persons and groups or in the form of passive supporters who can be activated. Another prerequisite is that the repression be widely publicised. The brutalities and indignities which the Civil Rights marchers suffered were nothing new in themselves — similar (and worse) indignities had long been the lot of blacks in the rural South — but the Selma marchers and others were carried out in a glare of publicity. White Americans all over the USA were literally forced to see for the first time what was normal practice in many areas of the South because this was widely, directly and dramatically publicised by press and television. It is well-known to psychologists that people fail to perceive what they do not like to see and the point of communicating information about repression is precisely to break through this 'psychological blindness'. One may speculate how the German extermination program for Jews might have been affected had the German population – and others – been forcibly made aware of what was happening.

2. THE EFFECT OF MASSIVE REPRESSION

While it has been suggested that limited repression by a more powerful opponent can sometimes function to the advantage of the resistance, the case of massive repression is much more problematic. In studying resistance movements of various types we can find examples where massive repression has apparently worked (Hungary in 1956, East Germany in 1953, and South Africa throughout are fairly obvious examples) and others where it has not achieved its objectives (Vietnam, Algeria, the strategic bombing of German cities, the resistance of the Yugoslav partisans during World War II, etc.). The short answer is that it is not known exactly why resistance is broken in some cases and not in others. However, an examination of the social contexts in which heavy repression has been used may supply some insights.

In situations where it is believed that there are no alternatives to resistance on the one hand, and complete extermination on the other it is not unreasonable to expect the resistance to continue irrespective of costs. Thus the Biafrans who believed (rightly or wrongly) that the Nigerians were bent on a policy of genocide continued fighting even under rather desperate conditions. Some resistance movements (the Mau-Mau in Kenya for example) actually make a point of requiring of their members that they commit some act which would lead to their execution if they were caught by the enemy. This is one way of attempting to ensure that the resistance continues until the leaders decide to call it off. Similarly the Mafia network in the USA maintains loyalty by exterminating those who quit their 'resistance' movement. Under such conditions repression is of course useless.

The failure to break the morale of German civilians by the strategic bombing raids over German cities by the Allies in

World War II must have had rather different causes. One could argue that the policy failed because there was nothing that German civilians could do to stop or in any way effect the Allied missions and under those circumstances of intense threat and fear, and of complete powerlessness, social disruption sets in and individuals simply seek support and protection (physical and, even more so, psychological) wherever they can find it, and adjusting their emotional ties to fit this one overriding concern (Thornton, 1968). The fact that German authorities could provide some measure of protection (in the form of shelters, alternative accommodation, limited medical services etc.) while the Allies could provide none is probably a crucial factor in explaining why the civilians went along with the war effort in spite of it all. This factor would seem to be quite generally a limitation on the effectiveness of strategic bombing and other means of indiscriminate terror applied from outside. The results of surveys carried out immediately after the war point to the same conclusion. They showed that war-morale was not significantly different in German cities which had been heavily bombed and in those where bombing had been relatively light (see *U.S. Strategic Bombing Survey*, 1946).

Occupation alone is normally preferable to occupation *and* resistance if only a day-to-day perspective is adopted. On this assumption continued resistance is rational only if there is a realistic prospect of a change for the better — whether the complete discontinuation of occupation or the transition to a more acceptable type of occupation. It is only by introducing this time perspective that resistance in the face of massive repression becomes rational.

This is not to claim that resistance can only occur when, in the narrow sense, it is rational from the point of view of those who resist — a claim which it would be hard to maintain in the case of German resistance in the latter years of the last war. It only serves to emphasize the paramount importance of the prevailing international power relationships and the historical and geographical context within which the resistance takes place. Thus an important reason why resistance in the occupied territories grew during the latter part of World War II (at the same time as repression became fiercer) while it has collapsed each time in the post World War II eastern European countries is precisely that in the first case there was a prospect for change and hence a motive for enduring hardships and continuing to resist, while in the latter cases no such prospects existed once it had become clear that all the major powers were content to return to the previous *status quo*.

Thus far we have dealt with the effects of repression in general and most of the examples we have used have been of repression against resistance movements which have been violent in character. What then can be said of non-violent resistance movements? It seems highly plausible that the restraints on the opponent's use of violence (and the destructive effects which his use of violence would have upon himself) are more pronounced when non-violent methods are used because in this case it is extremely difficult for an opponent to justify the use of violent repression to himself and to others.

It is of course logically conceivable that an opponent will have no scruples about using violence against the non-violent but he would still have to consider the effect on world opinion, his own troops etc. Many acts of repression, both against the non-violent and against very limited violence, have been accompanied by rationalisations or excuses (such as the frantic Soviet search for 'counter-revolutionaries' in Czechoslovakia). One can only conclude that world opinion (or rather sectors of world opinion) have in fact been thought of as important in such cases.

Where massive repression is weakening the resistance *without* weakening the opponent's resolve to go on applying it, where the external situation offers no real hopes of change, and where the alternative (more or less complete submission) is not as bad as continuing the struggle, then it appears that the most sensible strategy is to call a halt before the resistance is crushed and hope that it can continue in a more subtle form. Indeed, the point about civilian defence adopted as a national policy by a small nation which, anyway, has only limited control over its fate, is not to see the resistance in terms of 'winning' or 'losing', but to try to influence the situation to the national interest by a more flexible and pragmatic approach.

3. SUMMARY AND CONCLUSIONS

Low levels of repression should in most cases serve to increase the solidarity of the resistance and attract more support from the uncommitted. This presupposes that there is a large reservoir of potential support for the resistance and that the repression is widely publicised.

This is on the assumption that cleavages in the society are perceived to be relatively unimportant in comparison with the cleft between occupier and occupied. If this is not the case divisions might be used by the occupier as happened in Belgium during both World Wars, when the Germans could exploit the demands of the Flemish-speaking Belgians for social, cultural and economic equality with the French-speaking half of the population. This factor has been emphasised by some writers as a salutary aspect of civilian defence: efforts towards reducing gross social inequality and injustice would become a necessary part of the defence preparations. Under these circumstances low level repression is more likely to cause divisions in the opponent's ranks and isolate him internationally than to crush the resistance.

On the other hand if employed, *massive repression,* seems much more likely to achieve its aims of disrupting the resistance. Its efficacy, however, is to a very large extent dependent on events external to the occupation as such. Repression may of course fail when directed against certain types of millenarian movements and movements with ideologies like those of the Kamikaze in Japan or of the Mahdi of 19th century Sudan. Though minorities might conceivably be found in modern industrial societies which hold, or could be made to hold, such ideologies, it seems most unlikely that this could provide a basis for a civilian resistance which must necessarily involve a large part of the population.

Repression may also fail where force is applied from without (for instance by bombing, blockade, etc.) so that selective terror, 'divide and rule' and co-optation cannot be employed and the *individual* resistance fighter (in contrast to the resistance movement as a whole) does not have the possibility of seeking protection and support by joining the enemy. This is not the case where the repression is 'internal' (resistance against a military coup, an occupation, etc.)

In the case of occupation of a country like Denmark repression would not be applied from without but from within, or it would be a combination of both. The high degree of direct contact with the opponent means that the leaders of the defence cannot decide to continue the resistance without the cooperation of the civilian population. Because it presupposes that the opponent gets access to the territory, civilian defence leaves the resistance open to the opponent's efforts at splitting it. It is in one sense a definite source of weakness for the defence, namely in respect to holding out, but it also provides a safeguard against the insanity of fighting for a lost (or unpopular) cause. Many authors have seen this as a 'democratic' virtue of civilian defence which military defence lacks.

Repression may also fail to achieve its objectives of control and compliance where the resistance believes that if it submits its members will face extermination. In an occupation it is hardly conceivable that the situation could be seen in those terms and if it were, civilian defence methods would at any rate be of no avail.

Finally, repression may fail when resistance is seen as being in some sense effective, i.e., when there are reasons to believe that pressure by the opponent will sooner or later be relaxed and that resistance will precipitate this development or affect its outcome.

This is by far the most complex factor to evaluate in relation to the occupation of one of the smaller Western European countries, mainly because the possibility of such an occupation seems so remote and the international context within which it might take place as well as its forms and aims are therefore hard to visualise.

In the case of an occupation from the East which is not followed or preceded by general war in Europe the main rationale for continued resistance would be to prevent the situation from developing into a new status quo with the line separating the blocks moved further to the West. If and when it became clear that the major Western powers could or would do nothing to reverse the situation and that the resistance did not pose enough of a problem to the occupier to make him desist, resistance would almost certainly be replaced by some form of accommodation so as to aim at protecting certain institutions and values, not at expelling the occupying power. This means that resistance would be de-escalated until a level is reached where the opponent ceases to use massive repression.

Even harder to imagine is the situation where a protracted conventional war between East and West is being fought. (The case of a major nuclear war is not worth considering in the present context because it can only result in the annihilation of the countries of Western Europe and because the outcome, anyway, can only be negatively affected by resistance, whether civilian or military).

In this type of conventional war non-cooperation against the occupation as such would be relatively unimportant because the occupation would mainly serve short-term strategic goals. Furthermore, the prospect that a Danish obstructive resistance against the military use of its territory would be able to continue in spite of massive repression seems very slight. It would certainly require that the importance of Danish resistance to the Western war effort were very considerable — and even then doubts could be entertained — or else that active resistance be seen as a precondition for influencing a post-war settlement.

Perhaps the most reasonable (or at least unreasonable) scenario is that of a discreet western take-over or of a military or military-backed coup under the imminent threat of a drastic change in Danish foreign and/or domestic policies. This could conceivably be accompanied by repression on the model of Hungary in 1956 or of Greece since 1967. However, so many factors (many of them relating to internal political conditions) bear upon the question of the ability of resistance to persevere in spite of massive repression, that it seems fruitless at this point to go into any detail. The principal factor, at any rate, is probably not the level of repression but the degree of political unity of the population.

It must be stressed finally that in this section we have only been considering the likely effects of repression on the *defence*, and by ignoring its effects (direct and indirect) on the *attacker* we have bypassed the question of whether repression is at all likely to occur and if so, which form it would take. This is discussed more fully in Chapter X.

We have seen that civilian resistance does not seem very likely to hold out for long against massive repression, but neither does it seem likely that massive repression would go on for any length of time if opposed by non-violent means only. In the long run the liabilities of such a policy are too great.

The possibility that massive repression may crush resistance is, needless to say, no argument for discarding civilian defence any more than vulnerability to nuclear attack is a sufficient argument for scrapping conventional military defence. That would be to confuse the conceivable and the likely. Besides, the prospects are equally low that a *military* defence effort could go on in spite of massive repression against the population.

CHAPTER VI

Resistance Against Occupation: The Battle of the Ruhr and the Occupation of Czechoslovakia

In this and in the next chapter four cases are considered in which non-violent strategies have been used as a form of national defence against opponents from within and from without. The first case — that of the Ruhrkampf is considered in some detail while in the others a more selective approach is used.

While the case studies included here provide some insights into both the potential strength and the problems of non-violent defence it should be remembered that in no case had civilian defence been planned in advance. There was rarely more than a commonsense understanding of the various social mechanisms involved, and there had been no education or training in civilian defence tactics; nor had the population been psychically prepared for resistance in such a situation. Non-violence was adopted in each of these cases, not out of a belief that it was in an absolute sense superior to violence (whether for ethical reasons or because of its general efficiency), but because in *those particular circumstances* it appeared to be the best choice.

1. THE BATTLE OF THE RUHR, 1923

The German resistance to the French and Belgian occupation of the Ruhr in 1923 provides examples of many of the non-violent methods which have been proposed in the literature; it also provides examples of counter-strategies which the opponent may employ, suggests how the two are inter-related and demonstrates how in this particular case, the resistance finally broke down as a result of these and other factors. For historical material the following account draws heavily on Sternstein's paper *The*

Ruhrkampf of 1923: Economic Problems of Civilian Defence (1967), where further details and extensive references are to be found.

The official justification given for the invasion by the French and the Belgians was that Germany had defaulted voluntarily on war reparations payments. However, there seems to be little doubt that other considerations entered as well:

To enforce payment of reparations from Germany was only one of the aims pursued by France and Belgium. Another, no less important, was to prevent Germany from re-establishing its economy and threatening a war of revenge. "Security" was the leading consideration of French policies. In 1919 the other Allies had refused to safeguard France's security by guarantees, and France therefore felt it had to look after its own security. To this end Germany's economy had to be kept down, by reparations on the one hand and territorial sanctions on the other. The Ruhr area with its rich coal mines constituted a natural complement to the iron ore of Lorraine, and the combination of both industrial areas was bound to give France the leading position in Europe that it wanted. France's long term political aims went further, and included support for Rhenish separation and the creation of a "Rhenish Republic" dependent on France: some influential groups in France wanted ultimately to destroy the unity of the German Reich by dissolving Germany into separate autonomous states. (Sternstein, 1967)

France and Belgium occupied the Ruhr in January 1923 with the ostensible aim of setting up a control commission of engineers and officials to ensure that reparation payments would be forthcoming. Altogether some 90,000 troops were sent in to 'protect' the control commission. The occupation did not end until June 1925 when the former allies agreed to implement the Dawes plan according to which reparation payments were to be conditional on Germany's economic solvency — a principle not upheld by France and Belgium in 1923. The Ruhrkampf itself, that is to say active and passive resistance to the occupation lasted some nine months, from January 1923 to September 1923, although the period of effective resistance was shorter than this.

WAR WITHOUT WEAPONS

a) The Course of the Resistance

The Berlin Government's initial proclamation provided broad directives to the population of the occupied Ruhr which corresponded to Ebert's approach of 'working on without collaboration' as previously described. The occupying forces were on no account to be cooperated with, their orders were to be disobeyed and the Berlin Government was to remain the sole legitimate authority. Within this broad framework the various sectors of the population such as the civil servants, trade unions and shopkeepers evolved their own specific methods of resistance.

During the first few weeks there were a great many 'symbolic' demonstrations against the occupation. Four days after the occupation began there was a thirty minute general strike in the Ruhr and the performance of Wilhelm Tell at the municipal theatre in Essen 'developed into a demonstration of the national will to resist' (*Ibid.*). The response of the occupying powers to the massive disobedience of orders was to apply what we called 'limited' repression such as banishment, fines and imprisonment. As might have been expected this created a still wider and more intense support for the resistance. As Sternstein notes of the aftermath of the Mainz court martial in which six representatives of the mining industry were sentenced to pay heavy fines for refusing to obey the orders of the occupying powers: 'Their return to Essen developed into a triumphant procession, with crowds gathering along the railway line and at the stations.'

As noted, the form that non-cooperation took, varied considerably from one trade or sector to another. The mine owners, for example, considered, but decided against pre-emptive sabotage – the flooding of the mines – and also against the trade unions suggestion of a general strike. Their response consisted mainly in refusing to obey all orders of the occupying powers.

The resistance of the mine owners was in essence legalistic; in obeying instructions from the legitimate government in Berlin, they were disobeying the orders of the occupying powers. This resulted in a series of courts martial, which, however, did not secure the compliance the occupying powers wanted. The next step of the French was to forbid and effectively prevent the export of coal to the unoccupied areas of Germany and to require the coal tax and other revenues normally paid to the German Government to be paid to them. Defaulters were court-martialled and sentenced. The workers struck in sympathy but to no avail. Despite disruptions production in the Ruhr remained around seventy per cent of the normal level and the surplus which was normally exported was stockpiled. The occupying powers were unable to remove this as transport workers refused to transport coal to France or Belgium. Not before March, when a skeletal rail service was restored, were the occupying powers able to switch from using indirect pressures and instead to occupy the mines one by one. Despite the resistance from the workers the stockpiled reserves were loaded and sent abroad.

Resistance in the transportation sector was linked to that in the mining industry. In response to the strikes of the transport workers the occupying powers attempted to close down the whole rail and water transportation system. They eventually succeeded despite resistance from the workers. Later attempts to restore a skeletal service were obstructed by non-violent sabotage of rolling stock, engines, etc., but with only partial success. Using foreign labour and a Franco-Belgian railway administration brought in especially for that purpose, the occupying powers managed to restore a limited rail service. Collaboration with this administration was minimal (less than three per cent of the Ruhr railway employees) and the civilian population boycotted the few passenger trains that were eventually put into service.

Public officials in the civil service and local and provincial administrations were more constrained by instructions from the Berlin government than were the trade unionists, the press and other groups. Resistance lay primarily in refusing to obey the orders of the occupying powers and this led to mass deportations, arrests and fines. For failing to salute foreign officers, police officers were banished in such great numbers that for a while the area was virtually without civilian law enforcement.

The resistance of the press took the form of refusing to obey censorship instructions and publishing even when banned. Initially, editors and publishers were simply 'warned' but this was swiftly followed by arrests, fines and imprisonment. Papers were banned many times only to reappear clandestinely under new names or under the names of papers which had not been banned.

Shopkeepers and other sections of the self-employed middle classes were among the last groups to join the resistance and for reasons presently to be considered were among the first to give up the resistance. Following refusals by shopkeepers, restaurant owners and others in the service trades to serve the occupying troops, many shops were closed completely by the occupiers. What they could not buy the troops often looted.

b) Methods Used by the Defence

No attempts were made to delay the invasion of the Ruhr. The invading troops were actually brought in on German trains. Symbolic activities such as protest strikes and demonstrations characterised the earliest stages of the resistance and not the *blitzkrieg* which Sharp advocates. Total non-cooperation was not attempted, there was no general strike (except the initial 'symbolic' strike), suggestions for flooding the mines and for a serious nation-wide strike of all mining workers were rejected in favour of Ebert's more legalistic and moderate 'work on without collaboration'.

'Schweikism' and go-slow tactics were probably used but have not been recorded by writers on the resistance. Sabotage of the defenders' own property on the other hand was used as a denial activity. Grimm wrote:

In one sense the passive resistance was an active struggle from the very start. For instance, when civil servants removed office furniture the French wanted to use, when they cut the light and telegraph wires, when industrialists and workers rendered railway engines, hoists, or stores of coke unusable, when railwaymen damaged signal boxes before surrendering them, when workers of the Rhenish-Westphalian power plants cut off supplies to the head-quarters of M.I.C.U.M. in Essen, which action resulted in a court martial and a fine for Director Bussman . . . all these may be considered as rather active engagements. (Grimm,1930, quoted in Sternstein, 1967)

Several writers including Sharp (1965) have suggested that if extensive non-cooperation fails to achieve its ends rapidly then a more flexible limited response may be adopted. This seems to have happened in the Ruhr 'From 11 January to 8 May the resistance had continued undiminished, now it was replaced by a more flexible mood and a certain willingness to compromise which lasted until the end of passive resistance on 26 September 1923.' (Sternstein, 1967).

Apparently, civilian defence methods aimed at undermining the opponent indirectly by conversion and appeals to conscience were not deliberately made use of. This is not to say that the impact of the resistance did not undermine the support for the Franco-Belgian policy in these countries and in others, only that this was not the concern of those most directly involved in the resistance who were absorbed by the immediate problems posed by non-cooperation. As might be expected the Government in Berlin had a wider strategic perspective and according to Sternstein 'the strategy of Cuno's Government was designed to achieve two ends: first, to damage the French economy by withholding coal and thus compelling the French to withdraw; and second to isolate France and Belgium morally and cause a rift among the Allies.' (*Ibid.*)

During the first phase of the resistance, from January until the 8th of May non-cooperation was genuinely effective and did frustrate the specific objectives of the opponent. Yet the costs of this success to the resistance were very high. Non-cooperation denied the use of facilities not only to the opponent but also to the resistance which, unlike the occupying powers, had only limited and diminishing access to outside resources. So with the paralysing of rail and water transportation which hit the civilian population more severely than the occupiers. Strikes and imprisonments cut production and put thousands on to the meagre unemployment pay which bought less and less as a result of the rapid inflation.

c) Breakdown of the Resistance

There is no single factor which caused the eventual breakdown of the resistance, rather a combination of factors. It is useful to consider these briefly. Repression by the occupying powers, which initially had caused great indignation and actually increased the resolve to resist, gradually began to take effect. Such controls were imposed on exports to the unoccupied parts of Germany that trade diminished and finally ceased altogether, depriving the Ruhr industry of its major market. The area became increasingly dependent on subsidies from the unoccupied areas of Germany which, themselves, were economically growing weaker. One important point, undoubtedly, relates to the expectations of 'success' in the long term, and the situation at the end of the first five months of the Ruhrkampf could hardly support the view that the resistance could achieve much by long-term perseverance. Non-cooperation had frustrated the immediate objectives of the opponent but the determination of the Franco-Belgian occupying powers seemed to have increased rather than decreased.

It is precisely in this situation when prospects seem to grow dimmer each month that a crack in the unity of the resistance can trigger off a reversal of the 'bandwaggon effect' which initially sustains and strengthens the resistance. According to Sternstein 'the turning point came with the trial of the Krupp directors and that of Leo Schlageter, who had dynamited railway lines to stop the transport of coal'. After this, he claims, the inner strength of the resistance had been broken.

Without disputing the importance of these trials, another factor, of perhaps greater importance, is hinted at in his account, namely, the failure of the retail trade boycott: ' . . . the boycott movement was the first to break. The retail trade, its members dependent entirely on themselves, proved to be the weakest point in the front line . . . economic necessity and in many cases, pure selfishness, broke barriers which had been erected against the occupiers.' There are good economic and sociological reasons why this sector of the population might be the first to crack. Lacking a collective insurance scheme like that of the workers and the reserve means available to the upper class they stood most to lose by self-imposed sanctions against troops who had ample money to pay for their goods and who were prepared to loot if shopkeepers refused to sell. In contrast to the class of petty shopkeepers and self-employed in the service trades with its individualistic outlook, the working class is more accustomed to, and organised for, collective struggles and its better organisation and more collectivist outlook provides a basis for normative group pressures to prevent individual 'backsliding'. The point is not, of course, that the shopkeepers' boycott was necessary as such to the resistance, but that in a situation in which the economic basis for resistance is rapidly deteriorating, where expectations for success are fairly low and where many continue to resist mainly because of social pressure, the first real crack in the 'front line' can cause a rout. The resistance is on the verge of collapse when its unity rests on little more than other peoples' belief in its existence.

Thus far we have noted two factors. First, a general deterioration in economic conditions which in addition to the repressive political and administrative measures of the authorities reduced the ability of the population to resist while at the same time lowering expectations of what might be achieved by the resistance. Second, in the climate of relatively low motivation the first 'breaks' can cause a fairly rapid dissolution of the resistance as the 'bandwaggon' effect operates in reverse — the failure of the shopkeepers' boycott and the intensification of repression signalled by the Krupp directors and Schlageter trials were the concrete manifestations of this in the Ruhrkampf.

Sternstein notes two other factors: the over-organisation of the government's aid policies seems to have contributed to the general reduction in ability and motivation to resist, and sabotage which acted as a catalyst to the rapid breakdown of the resistance during its last phase (May/June to September).

The Government was 'too far removed from the scene of the battle to have any immediate conception or experience of the situation'. The complicated and bureaucratically organised relief measures were so slow in taking effect and inflation so rapid that often financial relief, by the time it arrived, was worth only a fraction of its original value. Sternstein claims that this 'over-organisation' was an important factor in undermining the economic base of the resistance. However, inflation in Germany at this period was so sever that one doubts that even a perfect distribution system would have made much difference.

Sabotage may be seen as a factor accelerating the dissolution of the resistance movement once its 'inner strength' had been lost. During the first phase of the resistance when unity was strong, sabotage activities apparently caused little adverse reaction from the civilian population — indeed they were publicly supported by the Cuno Government and Sternstein notes of the execution of Leo Schlageter that he was regarded as a "martyr of nationalism." However, after the beginning of May (which Sternstein sees as the turning point of the resistance) the public reaction to sabotage had become more negative. At Whitsun the Government in Berlin and the Reichswehr withdrew their support for sabotage and provincial governments denounced specific acts of sabotage, The sabotage of the Hochfield Bridge in which ten soldiers were killed led to savage reprisals and to the introduction of a widespread ban on road traffic which one writer claimed heralded the end of passive resistance. Thus acts of sabotage in a period in which the resistance was on the wane resulted in an acceleration in its decline, while serving no useful purpose. Indeed it is not clear that sabotage ever did serve a useful purpose. According to Sternstein acts of violent sabotage ' . . . had been of little effect and had hardly interrupted the lines of communication of the occupying powers to France and Belgium at all'. They also caused some reversal of sympathy for the passive resistance which had been building up abroad.

Whereas there seems to be some disagreement in the different accounts about the turning point in the struggle there is little doubt that after the Hochfield Bridge incident the resistance crumbled very rapidly indeed. In fact it is not at all clear that the non-cooperation which went on in various sectors was a form of resistance at all. In August, Sternstein writes, '. . . industry was in a state of near collapse and *had* to dismiss all personnel.'

The Government which replaced that of Cuno on 12 August 1923 was unequivocally committed to resuming reparations payments but was attempting to bargain over the conditions under which these might begin. However, conditions in the Ruhr were by then so desperate — 'the country was racked by hunger, riots and Communist and separatist risings' — that Germany had to yield unconditionally. Passive resistance came officially to an end on 26 September 1923.

d) Divisive Tactics of the Occupant.

The Ruhrkampf also provides clear examples of the use of various tactics by the occupier.

Broadly speaking the 'divide and rule' methods which may be used by an occupying power are the counterpart of what we have called 'undermining activities' when they were used by the defence. The positive sanction approach to undermining the occupant (by the selective use of rewards) finds its counterpart in rewarding particular sections of the resisting population in the hope of creating divisions. In the Ruhr the occupying powers were anxious to break the united front of employers and employees. Sternstein writes of the workers who resisted: '. . . *if* they were arrested at all, workers were treated more

leniently by court martial than employers or civil servants . . .
The authorities set up soup kitchens and shops; but the population
recognised their ulterior motive and refused to make use of this
aid.'

A similar tactic is to tolerate and encourage existing splits
In the late states of the struggle 'Communists and separatists
terrorised whole cities, The occupation authorities tolerated,
and in many cases, secretly encouraged them in the hope that
they would break the morale of the population'. Yet another
technique, well known in the field of industrial relations, is the
use of strike breakers — in this case the introduction of Polish
and Czech labourers and Franco-Belgian administrators to run
the railways. Such tactics are of little utility against a firmly
united resistance. As resistance weakens, so divide and rule
tactics become more and more effective.

c) Success or Failure of the Resistance

Some observers might see the Ruhrkampf as evidence of the failure
of civilian defence methods because the resistance was eventually
broken. Others, more sympathetic to the idea of civilian defence
might argue instead that *if* positive influence techniques had been
used instead of negative ones, *if* the resistance had been better
prepared and so forth, then the resistance might have succeeded.
Such arguments are to our mind much too crude because they
fail to see the complexity of the various objectives of the
resistance and of the occupiers, and fail to take into account the
secondary and the long-term effects of the resistance. In the end
these attempts to classify a resistance movement as success or
failure are merely ways of forcing complex historical occurrences
into oversimplified and utterly uninteresting categories. The
interesting thing is instead to analyse the domestic and international consequences of the resistance, and to ascertain what can
and what cannot be achieved.

Who won the war of the Ruhr? The question cannot be
answered unequivocally. There is no doubt that Germany was
forced to her knees and had to accede to the reparation
demands. But, when American representatives were included
in the committees, the question of reparations, against
Poincaré's original intention, was taken away from the
jurisdiction of the Reparations Commission, an organ of the

Versailles Treaty, and reconsidered by a wider international body on the basis of solely economic considerations. France's unilateral action resulted in a resurgence of world-wide sympathy for Germany. By the resistance of the population of the Rhine and the Ruhr, Germany's moral isolation was pierced. Most important of all, France failed to achieve her political goal, the separation of the Rhineland from the rest of Germany. Instead the Dawes plan, which resulted from the war of the Ruhr, was to become the first step on the road which led Germany out of political isolation and to Locarno and the League of Nations. (Erdmann, *see* Sternstein, 1967)

2. THE OCCUPATION OF CZECHOSLOVAKIA, 1968

'The Czechoslovak resistance against the August 1968 invasion by the five Warsaw Pact armies was the most dramatic case of non-violent action against foreign aggressors that the world has ever known. For six days following the invasion the Czechs and Slovaks openly defied the invaders, disobeyed their orders, refused all cooperation, and argued with them in an attempt to undermine the troops' reliability and internal morale. This disciplined and astute campaign of civilian resistance was the clearest case yet of the type of response to military attack which forms the subject of this book.' (Roberts, 1969a — introduction to the revised edition of *Civilian Defence*).

The Czechoslovak resistance has aroused great interest among protagonists of civilian defence and also in more conventionally oriented military circles such as the Rand Corporation (see Menges, 1968) and the Swedish Board of Psychological Defence, 1969). This interest had tended to centre around the technical conditions of the resistance (particularly the function of the radio, *Ibid.* and Hutchinson, 1969) and its tactical forms, i.e. the specific non-violent methods used (e.g., Ebert, 1969; Winkler, 1969).

There are several levels at which one may try to learn from the Czechoslovak experience. First, the events in the week immediately following the invasion demonstrated that the non-violent methods can work and that under suitable circumstances they can prevent the occupant from achieving his immediate aims. Below we shall consider some of these factors which made the resistance as forceful as it was.

Although the non-violent resistance was a powerful weapon in the first week, it is equally clear that its long term results were modest. This is due to two factors, each of which would have been a sufficient cause on its own. First, some at least among the long term goals of the Soviet Union were of such overriding importance that no resistance, however strong, could have weakened the Soviet determination, and second, the resistance did not last very long. Already after a week the process of erosion started.

Despite the fact that the Czechoslovak resistance, given the form it was to take, namely that of a national defence, was bound to fail under those particular political and international conditions it is nevertheless worthwhile to consider which factors contributed to its erosion as this experience might be useful in possible future less desperate situations.

a) Background to the Invasion.

Events during the occupation will be known to most and have been well documented by others (Roberts, 1969a, and 1969b; Windsor, 1969; Menges, 1968; Ebert, 1969; Winkler, 1969; etc.). Here we will simply deal with some aspects of the background to the invasion which clarify the political context and the aims of the Soviet Union, because a knowledge of the latter factors is a precondition for a discussion of the form and the course of the resistance and of its success or defeat.

The change of leadership in Czechoslovakia in January 1968, the political ferment during the year, the liberalisation of the media and the publication of the Action Programme in April were all part of a process which must have contributed to the creation of realistic fears in the Soviet Union that a crucial link in the chain of buffer states was potentially unreliable. Furthermore, despite Soviet pressure there were signs that the Czechoslovak leaders were in the process of losing control of the development and were either unwilling or unable to contain the demands for further liberalisation, decentralisation and autonomy. In Prague as well, the leaders seem to have been interested in applying the brake as conditions were beginning to look more like revolution than evolution. At the May plenum of the Party Dubček emphasised the dangers of what he called 'anti-socialist tendencies' for the process of democratisation and his attitude towards the 'conservative' elements remaining in the Central Committee was noticeably more moderate than his speech a month earlier (James, 1969). Despite constant pro-testations of unconditional support for the Warsaw Pact and constant affirmation of Czech adherence of Marxism-Leninism there was a real risk that the situation might eventually com-pletely escape the control of the Soviet Union, and the 14th Party Congress, scheduled for September could well have led to the complete emasculation of the remnants of the Party's pro-Moscow membership.

Whether Soviet policy is seen as essentially defensive or as essentially expansionist it is obvious that the maintenance of the East European buffer states — in particular those interposed between Western Germany and the USSR — constitutes a military interest so decisive to the Soviet Union that on this issue no compromise is possible. Twice in this century Russia has been attacked from Central Europe and the immense losses in the last war — twenty million dead, perhaps even more, — was the price paid for securing the Western frontiers. Seen in this light the demands for greater autonomy in Eastern Europe are only a secondary and, in a historical perspective, a temporary problem. The Soviet Union does not wish to see the present arrangement in Eastern Europe upset:

' . . . just because, as they see it, a few economists and politicians in Prague have caught a glimpse of the bright lights of western Europe. In their military and economic system Czechoslovakia has a key position. It is a workshop where a lot of Russian and East European raw material is processed; the country's territory forms a tunnel leading from Western Europe directly to the Soviet Union.' (Zeman, 1969).

The potential political and economic effects of the Czechoslovak experiment were equally serious for the Soviet Union because in the long run they might spread to other East European countries and perhaps even to the Soviet Union itself. The economic reasons favouring a change in the relations of production, a de-centralisation of decisions, and greater participation by the workers would sooner or later become equally pressing in other countries of Eastern Europe, and make them similarly interested in finding their own 'road to socialism'. Hungary had already embarked on a programme of economic reforms similar to those in Czechoslovakia. There had been political unrest – especially among students – in Poland; Rumania was openly critical of Soviet policies and there had been general resistance to attempts to increase economic integration in Eastern Europe through Comecon. Moreover, trade relations between Czechoslovakia and the USSR were very disadvantageous to the former and there is little doubt that Czechoslovakia would have derived considerable economic benefit from a greater trade with Western Europe.

Soviet foreign trade statistics give an idea of the situation. According to a summary in *Analyses et Documents* (6 March 1969) the Soviet Union paid on average thirty-five per cent less for goods bought in Czechoslovakia than it would have had to pay if similar goods had been bought in the West. At the same time Czechoslovakia had to pay thirteen per cent more for goods bought in the Soviet Union than would have been the cost of importing the same goods from the West. Prices were thus extremely unfavourable for Czechoslovakia. Nevertheless Czechoslovakia had an export surplus to the Soviet Union which by 1966 had risen to 8 million DM. At non-discriminatory prices, however, the surplus would have been 5.6 *billion* DM. The loss incurred in this way corresponds to eleven per cent of Czechoslovakia's national income.

Nor is this all. Even with the prevailing very unfavourable price structure Czechoslovakia has a permanent export surplus to the Soviet Union, i.e., a growing claim upon the Comecon Bank in Moscow. From 1960 to 1966 this credit rose by an amount corresponding to 2 billion DM and the resulting total Czechoslovak investment in Eastern Europe is estimated at 14 billion Czech Crowns. The credit being in Rubles and the Soviet Union having refused to give Czechoslovakia a 'loan' in hard currencies this surplus can only be used for purchases within the Eastern Bloc.

For the Czechoslovaks then, in addition to desires for greater political autonomy *vis à vis* the Soviet Union there were real economic advantages to be gained and West German business interests were very much in evidence during the Prague Spring.

Within the Soviet Union too there was a risk of contamination: the economic liberalisation for industry, political and cultural liberalisation and the abolition of censorship for the intellectuals and decentralisation for the various ethnic minorities of the Union.

In view of all these factors it is hard to escape the conclusion that no form of resistance which the Czechoslovaks might possibly have offered could have succeeded in gaining the form of autonomy they were seeking. While it is undoubtedly true that the strength of the resistance caught the Russians off balance there is no reason to believe that foreknowledge of it — or the expectation of an even stronger resistance — would have had any decisive effect on Soviet determination. It is also hardly conceivable that the Soviet leaders were not aware of the short term costs of the invasion in terms of world opinion in general, in terms of the allegiance of Communist parties abroad, of the cohesiveness of NATO, etc., but these costs must have seemed negligible in comparison with the possible costs of not intervening.

The point of this somewhat lengthy digression into the political, economic and military context in which the invasion took place is simply to stress that an understanding of the objectives and long-term interests of the opponent is crucial to an evaluation of the potential effectiveness of any defence policy — whether military or non-military. In a different political context, in another country at another time, where major interests of the USSR were not involved, a consideration of the indirect and direct costs of invasion might be sufficient to deter it; in the event of such an invasion, methods like those employed by the Czechslovaks might at least have assured the defenders of a substantially better negotiating position. Indeed the 'failure' of the Czechoslovak resistance should probably not be explained in terms of a lack of familiarity and expertise in the field of civilian defence but rather in terms of a gradual realisation within Czechoslovakia of the nature and extent of Soviet interests.

b) Unity of the Czechoslovak Resistance.

As several authors have noted, the initial response to invasion and occupation is usually one of confusion and despair. However, in contrast to many past invasions, the Czechoslovaks had not had the demoralising experience of a military defeat. Moreover, morale and the belief in the feasibility of effective action had been strengthened by the previous political victory over the hated Novotny regime.

It was suggested above that one contributing reason for the Warsaw Pact invasion was the belief that the leaders in Czechoslovakia were losing control. The Czechoslovak leaders themselves seemed to be aware of the dangers inherent in the speed and manner in which the democratisation process was progressing. The majority of the people, however, were probably too deeply involved in internal reforms to take much notice of possible external responses to the process. Within the country, workers, intellectuals and other key groups found a new identity in working towards the somewhat vague ideals of 'socialism with a human face' and in destroying the crumbling edifices of the previous regime. The invasion itself came as a complete shock to them, creating a feeling of intense moral outrage which further unified the nation. A realistic assessment of the prospects of resistance would not have justified much optimism, but there is little evidence that the Czechoslovaks' initial response was made in these terms. Indeed, the resistance seems to have been primarily an emotional reaction to the frustration of expectations which now seemed unlikely to be implemented.

One major prerequisite for the unified resistance which was to develop must, of course, be sought in the breakdown of divisions within Czechoslovak society in the months preceding the invasion. As an element in the democratisation process, the rifts inherited from the Novotny regime had to some extent been bridged, those in particular between the Czechs and the Slovaks, and those between the various classes: workers, students, intellectuals, bureaucrats and so forth.

The attitude towards the 'old guard' was also very different from those 'purges' which have accompanied the rise to power of other regimes. Ebert (1969) notes that '. . . the reformers won the day without creating a lasting polarisation between reformers and dogmatists. . . . The absence of collaborators was due not least to the fact that even inveterate Stalinists had no reason to be afraid of the reformers.'

The first phase of the resistance was marked by the symbolic activities which, as previously noted, have the purpose – or at least the effect – of creating a moral community, a feeling of 'belonging', and, if necessary, a foundation for group sanctions and social boycott. Thus the main function of the 14th Extraordinary Party Congress which met secretly in a factory was symbolic in that it voted in an even more liberal Presidium than that which the Russians could have feared from the Party Congress in September, moreover it voted overwhelmingly for the Dubček line. It denounced the invasion and rejected the Soviet claim that the intervention had been to save Czechoslovakia from counter-revolution. News of this and other important meetings were relayed over the 'free radio' networks. The radio similarly played a decisive part in bringing about the symbolic fifteen minute general strike on 23 August. The wearing of rosettes in the national colours also demonstrated the extent of solidarity and probably had an important impact in reassuring and supporting those who were wavering (Winkler, 1969). Such actions are clearly *symbolic* of resistance and their direct effect on the opponent is marginal. Instead, they build up and sustain the enthusiasm and solidarity of the resistance. In the first days the success must be considered to have been complete since it was impossible for the Soviets to find anyone who would admit to having asked for assistance from the Warsaw Pact in putting down the 'counter-revolution'. The fact that many Czechoslovaks during recent years have moved towards accommodation and, in some cases, outright collaboration suggests that it was the moral and social climate rather than universal and wholehearted support for the resistance which prevented collaboration in the first few weeks;

> . . . the massive, visible and continuing resistance acts as a warning to potential collaborators, either opportunists or the few who might have ideological reasons, a warning that the situation is still open and that the Soviets aren't guaranteed a victory yet. (Menges, 1969)

Some writers have sought to account for the fact that the Czechoslovaks did not turn to violence by referring to a Czech tradition for passive resistance or to a revulsion against the violence of the Novotny regime. Without denying that these factors may have had some effect it nevertheless seems more plausible to assume that the Czechoslovaks simply heeded the explicit instructions to avoid violence at all costs which the leaders and the radio were constantly reiterating, and that they correctly saw the futility of violent action in those circumstances. There were occasions when certain elements — especially amongst the young — wanted to turn to violence but in all cases they were dissuaded. Here too the cohesion of the resistance is crucial. This cohesion was in a way the most potent weapon of the Czechoslovaks and violence in defiance of the wishes of the leaders or of the majority would merely have split the resistance without achieving anything worthwhile. Furthermore, violent resistance would have made the Soviet claim of counter-revolution more credible, and the experience from the East German uprising of 1953 and the Hungarian revolt of 1956 can have left no illusions about the likely consequences of violent confrontation.

The resistance continued after the 'compromises' of the Moscow Agreement of 26 August but it never regained the strength and enthusiasm which had characterised the first six days. As Roberts (1969) noted, the slow dismantling of the Dubček revolution was 'an orderly retreat not an abject capitulation'. The Soviet response to the resistance and the way it gradually eroded it are considered later.

c) Importance of the Communication Media.

In contrast to the heavy emphasis on technological aids in military defence thinking, civilian defence writers have only occasionally paid any attention to them (Ruge, 1965; Galtung, 1967). In Czechoslovakia, however, the importance of radio, television and the press for the resistance was so evident that it has given rise to a number of studies (e.g.,Hutchinson, 1969, and Swedish Board of Psychological Defence, 1969).

The first question which arises is of a purely technological nature. How can a radio or television network be constructed and operated without being traced, jammed or otherwise silenced? This is no place to dwell upon technical details. Suffice it to say that there are countless ways of making detection more difficult, even with stationary transmitters. One possibility is to broadcast from several stations at once or in rapid succession (in Czechoslovakia, at one time, twelve different transmitters were assembled into such a coordinated network). Detection can be made more difficult but it cannot be completely prevented, and any system will necessarily have a limited life-span, unless the transmitters are located abroad. In the latter case, however, it is more difficult to provide the radio network with news, and much easier to disrupt its broadcasts by jamming.

Normally it will require extremely powerful noise transmitters to jam programs coming from inside the country itself, but in principle it is of course always possible. In addition to the relative power outputs of the respective stations jamming depends on the relative distances from the receiver to the signal transmitter on the one hand, and to the noise transmitter on the other, and it is therefore quite easy to drown foreign broadcasts in noise. It should be stressed, however, that there can be other reasons than the technical ones for not jamming transmissions. In particular there is the undesirable political and psychological effect for the occupant that if he jams he implicitly admits that he had no control over the situation and hardly expects to gain it.

Another problem of a technical nature has to do with the supply of information to the radio itself. Menges (1968) describes how the communications network operated:

The key was the combination of activist organisation, code names and the link with the telephone. Closing the internal telephone system would have brought the economy to a standstill, and this the Soviets weren't yet prepared to do. Tapping and tracing all the lines was technically impossible, and informers or prisoners had not yet provided the keys to the main radio-telephone hook-ups — which in any case, changed almost daily. As a result, informants would call designated relay stations, i.e. a person sitting by a telephone, with any news of interest. The relay person would filter this information to avoid duplication etc. then call a telephone watcher at one of the secret radio stations. There would be the usual news reporting system checks for accuracy, and then the editor would decide what to broadcast.

For external news each radio station had two normal short-wave monitors of which one was listening in on the western and the other on the eastern broadcasts.

Thus two short-wave radios and the telephone, plus informants and twenty-four hours of coverage created a far more informed dense and faster communication network than is customary even in the most news-saturated Western cities. (*Ibid.*)

There is no doubt that this system was entirely improvised, although it benefited from the fact that the Czechoslovak radio system had been a very decentralised one (Hutchinson, 1969), and even though it is to be expected that future invaders will be better prepared than were the Warsaw Pact troops, and that they

110

will certainly not let the first two days go by without attempting to silence the radio, there is nevertheless no reason to believe that one could not secure a few weeks 'free' broadcasting time in future emergencies (if the defence is also well prepared).

In various ways the radio served as a substitute for many of the functions of the State. Apart from providing information it gave direction and transmitted the decisions of the leadership to those who were to carry them out. After the leaders had been arrested and the public buildings and government offices had been occupied the radio served on a few occasions as a link between the civil servants. Thus, on 22 August it broadcast an appeal from the Minister of the Interior to the police and others not to follow any instructions from the Deputy Minister of the Interior, Salgovic, who was thus in effect dismissed. Similarly the transmission of the registration numbers of cars of the Soviet secret police functioned as a substitute for a police action against them. To the extent that communication within the public adminstration does not require secrecy the radio seems able to play an important part in keeping this institution going (or, more precisely, it seems to be a possible substitute for it). The openness itself, i.e. the fact that the entire population is able to listen in, also means that orders will be carried out even in those cases when a civil servant somewhere in the chain is unreliable.

Nevertheless, the most important role of the radio is undoubtedly in securing the participation of the total population in the resistance. By keeping everyone informed of what goes on it prevents all sorts of rumours from circulating and gives an authoritative version of the facts. Each participant knew whether in his active resistance against the occupant he could count on that protection which comes from belonging to the majority. The feeling of isolation and insecurity which is the occupant's best instrument for obtaining collaborators was kept at a minimum, and political activists as well as the masses, by being continually informed through the radio of their own acts, were made to feel that they were accomplishing something and were part of a community. Unambiguous and comprehensive information and the feeling of being able to achieve something are undoubtedly the main prerequisites for maintaining morale and unity.

d) Undermining the Resistance: The Soviet Strategy.

There is little doubt that the Soviet decision to intervene in Czechoslovakia was taken at very short notice and enacted within a matter of days. Throughout the "spring" the Dubček reforms had been the subject of constant vilification in the Eastern press, but at the meeting in Bratislava on 3 August the Czech leaders apparently managed to convince their Soviet colleagues of their willingness and ability to control the situation, for after the meeting the anti-Czechoslovak press campaign abated almost completely, and on the same occasion it was announced that the last remaining Pact forces would be withdrawn from Czechoslovakia.

However, just a week before the invasion the propaganda offensive was taken up again with renewed intensity. There are many possible explanations for this. In the intervening period (3 to 14 August) the new Draft Party Statutes had been published which stressed the continuation and consolidation of the Dubček reforms. In the same period the Czech journal *Literani Listi* had attacked the Russian interference in Czechoslovak internal affairs and the Yugoslav and Rumanian Presidents — both notorious for their autonomy from Moscow in external affairs — visited the country and were welcomed effusively in Prague. It is also conceivable that undertakings had been given to the Warsaw Pact allies in Bratislava which have not yet become known and which Czechoslovakia failed to carry out.

The haste with which the operation was carried out probably goes a long way towards explaining why the occupying powers were so unprepared for the political problems they were to encounter. The powerful popular resistance was clearly a surprise and it had obviously not been foreseen that it would be impossible to set up a government of collaborators, and that the radio and the press would try to continue in spite of the occupation.

Right from the start the Russians seem to have attempted to get rid of the leaders of the reform period. On 22 August there was apparently an attempt to set up a Quisling-government but the reaction which was building up rapidly throughout Czechoslovakia indicated that this would be politically impossible. Attempts to get President Svoboda to form a pro-Moscow government on the 22nd also failed as Svoboda indicated in his radio broadcast the following day. The Moscow discussions took place from 23 to 27 August. They were at least an important victory for the resistance in one respect, namely that the Czech leaders returned.

The text of these agreements was secret but the impression given at the time was that genuine concessions had been made on both sides. The Czechoslovaks agreed to the 'resignations' of some of the leading reformists, including the Deputy Prime Minister Ota Sik, the Minister of the Interior General Pavel and the Foreign Minister Hajek as well as the directors of the radio and television. More important, the active resistance was called off. On the other side of the table the Soviets seemed to have accepted parts of the reform programme, to have promised that the troops would not interfere in Czechoslovakia's internal affairs and to have recognised the legitimacy of the existing regime.

Whether or not it had been their intention throughout, it is clear at least that the Soviets rescinded their concessions in the deal one by one and thus were able gradually to regain complete (indirect) control over Czechoslovakia. Once the country had been occupied, the resistance had been officially called off and the ordinary 14th Party Congress had been pre-empted, the Soviets had time on their side. The Czechoslovaks could expect no help either from the West or from other East European countries and the Russians had on previous occasions shown their willingness to use tough methods if necessary.

In contrast to other resistance movements which have collapsed (the Ruhrkampf, for example) it was not physical repression or hardship which eroded the resistance in Czechoslovakia but rather the very fact of making concessions in the first place, the gradual abandonment by the Moscow government of its share of the concessions, the increasing Soviet pressure on the leadership, the gradual realisation of the futility of resistance against such a powerful and determined opponent, and the realignment of interests within Czechoslovakia, following the gradual realisation that the Czech spring had been an Indian summer.

Roberts sees the Soviet strategy in the following way:

. . . in subsequently demanding the implementation of all the promises that had been extracted [at the Moscow talks] the Russians played an astute game. Like all occupation powers, the Russians sought to work through local political leaders if at all possible. By doing so, they could use Czech unity against Czech aspirations. The remarkable unity of the Czech and Slovak nations in the period following the invasion was really no stronger than the leaders, because if the people tried to resist where their leaders had conceded, Czechoslovakia's strongest weapon, its unity, would have been undermined. The absolute necessity of unity explains why, despite numerous threats from students and workers to strike if concessions went too far, none of these threats was ever really carried out. To make the threat made perfect sense; to execute it would have introduced new stresses and strains into the Czechoslovak body politic (Roberts, 1969c).

In drawing on the reserve of trust and support Dubček retained with the population while the situation in Czechoslovakia was being normalised in accordance with their wishes, the Soviet leaders were able to use Dubček while he himself prepared the ground for his eventual and inevitable replacement. Expressive demonstrations of anti-Russian hostility occasionally took place in the months following the two Moscow agreements. On 7 and 11 November the *Czech* police used tear gas against demonstrators for the first time in decades. The demonstrations constituted a dilemma for the leadership for they would either have to repress them, thus losing the popularity and dividing the nation, or else there was the risk that the Soviet troops would take over the responsibility for law and order. Thus gradually the rulers were estranged from the population and destroyed that unity which had been the foundation and the precondition for the resistance in the first week after the invasion.

Since then the development has continued along the same path. The large demonstrations in March 1969 following the Czechoslovak ice hockey victory over the USSR led to violent censorship regulations and a tighter control over the Party. Dubček's replacement followed a month later. Attempts at weeding out the most recalcitrant persons, intimidating the rest and using informers to create a climate of fear and submission have continued unabated (see, for instance, Morgenthau, 1969, about the purges and intimidation in the educational sector).

There are still signs of sullen passive resistance in Czechoslovakia. A year after the invasion *Rude Pravo* described how workers were using 'go slow' and the pretense of ineptitude and how this was 'coldly calculated to achieve the disruption of the national economy', and the anniversary of the invasion was the occasion of large demonstrations in Prague. However, the impression is that these acts of resistance mainly serve as an outlet and completely lack political potency and effect — except, perhaps, in the direction of further repression.

c) Conclusion

It seems to us that it is not possible to conclude from the defeat of the Czechoslovak resistance the uselessness of civilian resistance in the general case, for there were at least two important factors which made the situation much more difficult in Czechoslovakia than it would have been in most other places. First, Czechoslovakia is for a number of reasons — of military strategy, of domestic policy and economic — of such decisive importance for the Soviet Union that in fact no compromise was possible. There was nothing which Czechoslovakia could have done, whether militarily or non-violently, to raise the Soviet costs of continued occupation to a level where they would matter and, of course, the possibility of conversion does not exist when the vital interests of the opponent are involved. The fact is that the Soviet Union has a complete monopoly of power within its sphere of influence, so that it was impossible to find anything but moral support abroad.

Under the given conditions it would hardly have been possible for the Czechoslovaks to avoid something akin to the Moscow agreements and these were after all only the beginning of the dismantling of a resistance which anyhow had no prospect of success. The agreements legalised the occupation, stopped the official resistance and introduced the first elements of a self-administered censorship. At this point the popular resistance was finished, for either the movement would split between those who followed the government's requests for cooperation with the occupant and those who continued to resist, or else the leaders would have to use all their authority to stop whatever happened to be the most extreme forms of resistance at each particular moment in order to safeguard unity. In either case the end result would be the same.

If one accepts the interpretation given above of the causes of the collapse of the resistance of the Ruhr then both examples illustrate how the complete unity of the resistance is the absolutely inescapable condition of its continuation, and how this unity itself presupposes that the resistance never exceeds what the weakest link in the chain can stand. In Czechoslovakia the leadership was the weakest link and in the Ruhr it seems to have been the small shopkeepers. This seems to be a factor of crucial importance in planning or in carrying through a non-violent defence: to get the 'rearguard' along has an importance which far transcends its direct contribution to the resistance.

It does not follow from what has been said that the Czechoslovak resistance was useless, and here again one must warn against the crudity of using the concepts of victory and defeat to describe the political consequences. If the costs to the Soviet Union were not large enough to prevent an active intervention or to repel it, they were heavy all the same. The Soviet Union intervened when it seemed clear that they were facing a situation which looked like the beginning of a revolution, but this does not prevent — indeed it may promote — the search for solutions which are more permanent than repression. This is what happened in the economic sphere in Hungary after 1956.

Nevertheless, if one takes an overall political perspective (rather than the more limited tactical perspective which characterises much of the work on civilian defence) there seem to be good reasons for directing more attention towards means for averting intervention in the first place rather than the ultimately futile (in this case) emphasis on tactics to resist invasion once it has occurred.

CHAPTER VII

Resistance Against Military Coups: The Algerian Generals' Revolt and the Kapp Putsch

The Kapp putsch of 1920 and the Algerian Generals' Revolt of 1961 are both examples of non-violent resistance which 'succeeded'. in the crudest sense of this word: both ended by the unconditional surrender of the insurgents, even though in both cases they had had the backing of the major part of the armed forces. The two examples are also interesting because they show how non-violent methods may be used against an internal military threat or against an external threat supported by the country's own military forces. In this case there are of course no military forces for the incumbent government to use and the resistance is therefore non-violent – or rather non-military – almost by necessity. In the case of coups, especially from the right wing, experience shows that the military are an unreliable ally for the government and the two examples to be considered below seem to show that non-violent resistance may constitute a rather promising substitute.

In the countries of North-Western Europe with their long record of internal stability, a military coup might seem a very remote possibility, but whether it is more or less remote than a foreign military attack is hard to tell. Political stability may be more apparent than real and it may be dangerous to rely upon it. In Northern Ireland, for instance, where the Unionist Party held power without interruption for half a century down to 1972, and where, until a few years ago, all signs pointed towards a smooth and gradual development, a forcible takeover by groups with fascist leanings is today far from implausible. In the same way the period of de Gaulle's Presidency was generally acclaimed as one of the most stable in recent French history until the events of May 1968.

A military or military-backed coup, with or without foreign support, does not, of course, come suddenly, out of the blue. On the other hand there does not seem to be any reason why the conditions for a military coup — those conditions which both make it possible and make it seem necessary from the point of view of certain groups — could not arise in the countries of North-Western Europe and it might therefore be useful to point out a few of the most obvious conditions.

A possible course of events might start with a reduction of tension in East-West relations, and hence in the feeling of external threat, and a greater tendency for division on domestic issues and for strikes, demonstrations and other forms of political unrest. An element in such a development is the increased uncertainty about the future of the armed forces, of the draft, of the NATO membership and of the scale of the defence establishment in general.

Under such circumstances, where political control is faltering, where the future is uncertain and established interests are threatened it is often the case that the police and the authorities 'overreact' and that police action contributes to creating and amplifying street disorders, instead of preventing and reducing them. This is what happened both in Paris in May 1968, in Greece and in Northern Ireland. In this way groups on the wings were able to provoke and to exploit tensions between the authorities and certain other sections of the population, and to make the maintenance of law and order appear in its other guise: as repression. In those cases where the authorities cover up the methods of the police the foundation is laid for political scandals, for the fear that they may come to light (Greece, Italy) and for political chaos once the confidence in the political institutions, in the politicians and in the authorities begins to crumble (Northern Ireland). If such a process is allowed to go on it is to be expected that large sectors of the middle class and of the right wing will demand a 'strong' government which can put an end to disturbances and insecurity, at least in a transitional period. This satisfies one of the conditions for a forcible takeover to succeed, namely that it must have a minimum of popular support. At this point only an acute opportunity will be needed where there seems to be an imminent threat against established ideologies and traditional interests and power relations such as an election which brings a militant left wing to power, creates a parliamentary deadlock or threatens to weaken the military decisively by substantial budgetary cuts or dismissals or withdrawal from NATO.

It was such a pattern of demonstration and protest, of repression, of an acute risk of a major political scandal and the necessity of pre-empting a safe electoral victory for the left wing which led to the colonels' coup in Greece. At short notice, conditions could become similarly ripe in Italy.

Although it can be reasonably maintained that in many countries the likelihood of a coup or of some other disruption of the parliamentary system is small and does not at present justify substantial counter-measures there are a number of other reasons why it is worth considering the experience of non-violent resistance against coups. This is so even if one arbitrarily limits the concept of security to the safeguarding of the country against external threats.

Firstly there are a number of technical lessons which may suggest ways of rendering a civilian defence more effective. These relate in particular to the question of cooperation and non-cooperation in the administration and the problem of legitimacy, i.e. the importance of maintaining a government or some other symbol of legitimate authority to unify the resistance. The number of coups which have been dealt with by non-violent means is much larger than the number of foreign invasions which have been countered in this way, and already for that reason the available experiences are much more useful.

Another reason for studying the experience of military coups is that a coup may be a discreet substitute for occupation or a preparation for it, foreign troops being called in later to help what has become the 'legitimate' government as a result of the takeover. Alternatively, occupation may be followed by the installation of a domestic regime by the occupying forces. Examples are numerous: collaborators' governments like Quisling's in Norway which are fabricated by the occupant, and externally inspired coups which are made to look like domestic takeovers such as the coup in Czechoslovakia in 1948 and the Saigon coups.

It must be stressed, however, that there is an important difference between a coup without external support on the one hand, and an occupation or a coup related to an occupation on the

119

other. In the latter case it is possible for the insurgents to draw on external resources and they are therefore not as totally dependent upon the cooperation of the population right from the start. While the mobilisation of the population is a *necessary condition* for effective resistance against occupation it is normally *sufficient* to make a coup collapse. The success of a coup is only undecided if, and as long as, there is substantial support for both sides.

1. THE ALGERIAN GENERALS' REVOLT, 1961

General de Gaulle had come to power in France 1958 with the support of the right and on the understanding that he would put an end to the war and retain Algeria for France. By the spring of 1961, it had become clear that de Gaulle was in fact going to relinquish French control over Algeria. To large sections of the officer class in the armed services, still rankling under the humiliating defeats suffered by the French military in Indochina this appeared an intolerable 'sell-out'.

The coup was led by four generals: Challe, Salan, Jouhaud and Zeller. It took place on the night of Friday to Saturday 21 to 22 April when the First Foreign Legion Parachute Regiment moved into the city of Algiers. Few shots were fired and during the whole period of the coup only one person is known to have been killed.

Most of the French forces, around half a million men, were in Algeria at the time, and most of the commanders rallied the rebel cause during Saturday and Sunday. A few loyal officers were arrested. Among those who were wavering or remained loyal to the government there was no willingness to fire on the insurgents. One of those who remained loyal, General de Pouilly, withdrew his forces from Oran when the rebels arrived to avoid a confrontation.

The French forces outside Algeria were few and on the whole not too reliable. The two army divisions in Germany, totalling little more than a tenth of the strength of the forces in Algeria, were led by right wing officers who had been stationed there to prevent them from creating trouble in Algeria. The head of the air force in France supported the putsch. Only on Monday night three days after the putsch, did the French commander in Germany declare his loyalty to the legitimate government in Paris.

It was believed at the time — although, predictably, denied by the leaders of the coup at their trial — that an airborne invasion of France was being prepared.

It was Sunday evening before General de Gaulle, and, a little later, Prime Minister Debré, broadcast appeals to the nation. It was commonly thought at the time that this long delay was an important reason why the insurgent Generals had succeeded so well in the beginning and had secured such wide support in the French army.

In his speech de Gaulle asked for non-cooperation: 'In the name of France . . . I forbid every Frenchman, and in the first place, every soldier, to carry out any of their orders'. Debré asked for a gesture more aimed at persuasion of the insurgents:

> . . . the authors of the Algiers coup . . . have planes ready to drop or land parachutists on various airfields [in France] as a preliminary to a seizure of power.. . . As soon as the sirens sound, go [to the airfields], by foot or by car, to convince the mistaken soldiers of their huge error. Good sense must come from the soul of the people and everyone must feel himself a part of the nation   (quoted in translation from Roberts, 1967d).

Being unable to rely on the military, de Gaulle and Debré had had to appeal directly to the population to resist attack on the metropolis. Airports were closed, vehicles were kept to hand to block runways if required, the *Gardes Republicaines* protected key buildings in the capital. A home guard was formed but never received arms, and a financial and shipping blockade was imposed on Algeria. On Monday, a one-hour strike by ten million workers demonstrated their solidarity with the Government and President.

Whether the risks of invasion were over-dramatised is open to question, at any rate the appeals for resistance had a considerable effect in inciting troops in Algeria to disobey. General Challe noted at his trial that ' . . . General de Gaulle's speech was making the waverers hesitate still further.' The dissident elements in the Army and particularly conscripts who did not share the political view of the putschists, engaged more in resistance by 'Schweik' methods than in open non-cooperation (which is severely punished in the Army):

Orders got lost, files disappeared, communications and

transport got tied up. The coup leaders had to waste forces they needed elsewhere — and might have used in an attack on Paris — to keep order in barracks and bases in Algeria (Roberts, 1967e).

Airfield runways were blocked, some pilots invented mechanical failures, others flew their aircraft out of Algeria. The resistance to the coup remained entirely non-violent in spite of de Gaulle's veiled call to resistance by 'all means' on Sunday and his explicit order to fire on the rebels on Tuesday evening. On the other hand it took the conscripts in the barracks in Algeria several days to realise that they could refuse to cooperate and to perceive the strength which non-cooperation gave them (Roberts, 1967d).

On April the 26th, four days after the coup, the First Parachute Regiment withdrew from Algiers, — the Generals Revolt had been defeated, virtually without a shot being fired.

2. THE KAPP PUTSCH, 1920

At the time of the Kapp putsch Germany was facing grave economic problems and was afflicted with large scale unemployment. The country was in a state of permanent political unrest, and disillusionment and apprehension about the future were rampant. The capitulation in 1918 and the accession by the Republican government to the unequal peace treaties and their clauses regarding war reparations were regarded by many as an act of treason against the Fatherland and the Army, and various right wing political factions were actively seeking the restoration of the Monarchy. The army had been much reduced in strength in accordance with the stipulations of the Peace Treaties and a considerable part of the disaffected military were being re-organised into *freikorps* and other voluntary and more or less unofficial armed bands and paramilitary corps. Several coups, both by the Right and by the Left, took place in the years following the war against the governments of the Länder and the Federal Government. Some were successful. Thus, a Rightist coup in Bavaria on the same day as the Kapp putsch succeeded and left this state virtually independent politically.

The Kapp putsch in 1920 is among the most frequently quoted examples of the successful use of non-violent methods. To all intents and purposes the coup had succeeded in the first place, but was subsequently defeated by lack of popular support and by effective non-cooperation. The following brief account is based mainly on Sharp (1965 and 1969) and Raloff (1937b).

The coup was directly provoked by the government's decision to disband the *freikorps*. On March 10th 1920 the extreme Right wing nationalists Dr Wolfgang Kapp and General von Luttwitz issued an ultimatum to President Ebert of the Weimar Republic, demanding new elections and rule by a cabinet of experts. Among the aims of the Kappists were the repression of Communism, the restoration of the Monarchy under Wilhelm II and the discontinuation of the dissolution of the armed forces under the terms of the Versailles Treaty.

Ebert rejected the demands and warned that any attempt to overthrow the Republic would be met by a general strike. It seemed clear by this time that the army — in particular the officer classes — was not unsympathetic to the idea of a Rightist coup. Kapp in fact received assurances that neither the armed forces nor the police would resist an attempt.

On March 12 the Kappists, supported by the five thousand strong Ehrhardt Brigade, a well-trained and well-armed *freikorps*, marched on Berlin without opposition from either army units or the police. The few officers who remained loyal refused to fight 'Reichswehr against Reichswehr'. On March 13 just before its occupation, the Ebert government fled Berlin, re-establishing the seat of the Government, first in Dresden and eventually in Stuttgart. Kapp declared himself Chancellor of the Reich and von Luttwitz was appointed Commander in Chief of the armed forces.

The Ebert Cabinet, backed by the Social Democratic Party, called for a general strike thus legitimising the spontaneous strikes which had broken out in Berlin on March 13. The authorities in the German Länder were instructed to refuse to cooperate with the illicit regime and to retain contact with the Ebert government in Stuttgart. An appeal from the social democratic members of the Government read:

. . . the strongest resistance is required. No enterprise must work as long as the military dictatorship of the Ludendorffs reigns.
Therefore, stop working! Strike! Strangle the reactionary clique! Fight by all means to uphold the Republic. Put all

123

mutual discords aside. There is only one way to prevent Wilhelm II from returning: the whole economy must be paralysed!

No hand must move! No proletarian must help the military dictatorship. The total general strike must be carried through! (Raloff, 1937b).

The general strike received the support of workers from all political and religious groups, although the Communists had at first refused to take part in it. The printers in Berlin went on strike after the seizure of two Berlin papers, which had supported the legitimate Government, and by March 14 the general strike was in full swing. No 'essential services' were exempted. The strike was particularly effective in the administration. Leading civil servants refused to run the ministries under the insurgents and the administration as a whole refused cooperation. In particular the regime found itself unable to draw upon the Treasury. According to a decree issued by the Government in Dresden civil servants who paid out public funds to the Kapp Government would be held personally responsible. Severe threats and forcible repression were used by Kappists against the strikers and some were shot. Particularly bloody confrontations between armed workers and rebel troops took place in Mecklenburg and Schlesien, but despite this the strikes continued to spread. The very narrow limits to the power of the insurgent government in Berlin became increasingly obvious. It could issue decrees and orders, but these were not being acted upon. The Kapp government made proposals for a compromise but these were rejected by the Ebert government on the 15th. Leaflets were showered over Berlin by plane with the caption: 'The collapse of the military dictatorship.'

The coup collapsed on May 17, after four days, In the morning security police in Berlin demanded Kapp's resignation. He resigned later that day and fled to Sweden. Von Luttwitz resigned as Commander in Chief in the evening while many of the other conspirators were fleeing Berlin, in civilian clothing. On the 18th the Ehrhardt Brigade, now under President Ebert's orders, marched out of Berlin. It subsequently took refuge in Bavaria under the new government there.

3. LESSONS AND CONCLUSIONS

The Kapp putsch is an example of total non-cooperation, of the non-violent *Blitzkrieg* which Sharp advocates as a first phase in the resistance. In contrast to the general strike in France which only lasted an hour and merely served as a demonstration, the German general strike was not meant as a symbol; it was used as a means of denying the Kappists any real political control. Many writers have stressed that to succeed, total non-cooperation must yield very quick results because it entails such large costs for the resistance. Faced, as was Kapp, with such a massive resistance there are in Ebert's view only two choices the coup leader can make. 'He can either relinquish authority altogether, as Kapp did after a few days of his militarily successful putsch in March 1920; or he can try to assert his authority with severe measures of intimidation.' (1967). It can be claimed that the reason for Kapp's defeat was his unwillingness, or his inability, to choose the latter course, but this, after all, amounts to saying that the non-violent campaign succeeded. The military leader, Ehrhardt, apparently wanted to break the strike by shooting trade union leaders and strike pickets, but did not find support for this.

The Kapp putsch was quite amateurish in design and execution, in contrast to the military efficiency with which the Greek 1967 coup was carried out. In Greece the first few hours and days of the coup were used to round up the political leaders and thousands of others who could have organised a resistance against the new regime. Kapp left the political leaders plenty of time to escape and set up a parallel government in another part of the country. It is similarly clear that if the Algerian generals intended to invade the mainland of France they should have acted much faster than they actually did. Both cases clearly point to the importance of having the original government continuing to function so that it can act as a symbol of legitimacy and as a rival authority. As Goodspeed (1967) notes 'the real tactical aim of those who are attempting a coup is . . . the government leaders. These must normally be either killed or captured.' If this does not happen, the conflict is likely to take the form of a dispute about who has the greater credibility, and the decisive factor becomes the bandwaggon effect noted earlier. It is therefore no accident that both coups were quite brief (both lasted for about four days). It is reasonable to assume that a more thorough analysis of coups than can be undertaken here could provide valuable understanding of the bandwaggon effect and of the factors affecting political wavering.

The events in Algeria provide a clear illustration of the difference between an occupation defence and a frontier defence. Those officers who remained loyal were unwilling to let one part of the Army open fire on another, and perhaps some among them were not too keen to take a clear stand against the coup before it was quite certain that it would be defeated. At any rate they withdrew their troops each time from those buildings and places which the rebels wanted to occupy, and in this sense there was no resistance. Concurrently, non-cooperation went on and constituted the real threat against the insurgents.

The two coups had this in common that there was no effective military resistance and that no threat to this effect would have carried much conviction. At the same time the non-violent resistance contributed to creating dissent among the conscripted soldiers, a process which would probably not have occurred to the same extent if military force had been used against the insurgents, thus welding them together.

It should also be noted that in both cases the insurgents were defeated by being *forced* to capitulate, not by any political conversion. Many among the participants in the Generals' Revolt in 1961, later joined the secret terrorist organisation, the OAS, and in Germany individuals like von Ludendorff, who seems to have been one of the conspirators in the Kapp putsch, were to be found as prominent figures in Hitler's abortive coup in Munich a few years later.

The most important conclusion to be drawn from the four examples we have considered in this and in the previous chapter is that in some cases civilian resistance does in fact seem to work in a *technical* sense. By this is meant that it is possible to create the group identity, the will to resist, the coordinated effort and the effective non-cooperation which this form of defence presupposes. The four examples do not permit generalisations about the conditions under which such resistance will arise because they have not been chosen with a view to being representative.

The fact that a particular piece of hardware is suitable as a weapon and works in a technical sense is, of course, no guarantee that it will promote one's political aims if used in some specific situation; similarly, the question of the *political effectiveness* of civilian defence is not answered by showing that in a *technical sense* it can be made to work. The problem of the political effects of non-violent resistance is a much more intricate one and one that cannot be solved in the abstract, i.e.,without taking account of the political context in which the resistance takes place.

Finally, it seems clear to us on the basis of three among the four cases considered that the non-violent methods cannot be dismissed offhand as ineffective, even when they are used in a direct confrontation with military means. In the case of Czechoslovakia, more distance from the events is needed before one can form a final judgement on the total effect of the resistance on conditions in Czechoslovakia, in the Soviet Union and in Eastern Europe in general; but in the other three cases it is clear that the non-violent methods, and particularly non-cooperation, had a definite impact on the final political outcome.

CHAPTER VIII

External Defence: Deterrence and Dissuasion

A major reason why recent writers have stressed the effectiveness of civilian defence as a means of struggle rather than its ethical superiority or its beneficial long term effects is that this makes it possible to compare the relative efficacy of civilian defence and military defence. By limiting the discussion to the question of combatting or defeating an attacker the hope was to make possible a dialogue between proponents of two approaches to defence which had a common goal.

All the same the dialogue never really materialised, and the proponents are still largely talking past one another. As technological development has gone on and has made weapons more destructive and war more insane, the orthodox argument for the continual reliance upon military means has changed. The emphasis is today much more on the ability of these means to deter an opponent from attack, and the ability to *conduct* a war is seen as a means towards this end. If, therefore, one wants to be able to compare non-violent and military defence systems on the premisses, exclusively, of the latter, then the central issue must be whether the former can compete as a means of *preventing* attack. This is a question on which the existing literature has very little to say, and the following remarks are therefore mainly intended to locate the problem.

In modern strategic terminology deterrence refers to that process whereby the opponent is prevented from attacking by being threatened with a retaliation which will impose so heavy a cost upon him that it exceeds any conceivable gains from the attack. Had this been all there is to it, it would have been clear already at this point that non-violent defence would be vastly

EXTERNAL DEFENCE: DETERRENCE AND DISSUASION

inferior to, say, nuclear forces, because the former only has a very limited capability for imposing costs on the opponent.

As is well known, three elements enter the 'calculation' which, supposedly, deterrence involves: the expected *gain* of the attacker, his possible losses from retaliatory attack, and the likelihood that retaliation will actually be implemented, the so-called *credibility*. Generally speaking, then, the idea is to make attack *less tempting* by affecting the costs and benefits of war. However, in a complete evaluation of' the possibilities of reducing the likelihood of war the question of reducing the *opponent's need to attack* must also be considered. This raises the questions of attempting to solve conflicts by prior negotiation, of reducing the opponent's apprehension that he himself will be attacked and so forth. To emphasise this wider perspective we use the word dissuasion to describe all those endeavours which, in times of peace, serve to make the opponent desist from attacking. Deterrence is that particular form of dissuasion which bases itself on the induced fear of the consequences of the attack.

1. THE FEAR OF AGGRESSIVENESS AND THE PREVENTION OF CONFLICTS

It is clear that the fears of the opponent that he will be the object of attack are directly related to a nation's offensive and retaliatory military capability, i.e. to that nation's ability to wage war outside its own territory. Fear of aggression from an opponent may be the rationale for a pre-emptive strike, fear of pre-emptive strikes becomes a reason for considering pre-pre-emptive strikes and herein lies the possibility of another of the vicious circles of contemporary strategic thinking, and a further example of the self-defeating character of the logic of deterrence The problem arises, not so much from the possibility of a retaliatory attack (if all ethical considerations are disregarded, that is) as it does from the offensive potential, and the difficulty is that, on the whole, it is the same military equipment, which is needed both for an offensive and for a defensive policy.

Where no offensive or retaliatory potential exists fears of military aggression are obviously reduced to zero and the notion of pre-emptive strike becomes meaningless. This has been one of the main arguments put forward for unilateral disarmament policies and of course also applies to civilian defence as the sole means of national defence.

It should not be assumed, however, that non-military 'external defence' capabilities cannot be seen as threatening by other nations. Where Sharp (1971) talks about 'accentuating the weaknesses' of totalitarian regimes by non-violent means he refers to an activity which would most certainly be perceived as 'subversion' — and thus as a threat — by such regimes. In a similar vein Galtung remarks on the 'provocation effect' of offensive non-military strategies (1967) and Schelling (1967) points out that 'the original conception of Communist conquest' was one of 'civilian offence'.

The lack of a military capability in a country where civilian defence is the sole means of defence implies that none of the opponent's strategies designed to destroy *military* defence capability need be used. Civilian defence is useless against nuclear attack, aerial bombing etc. but since there is no military resistance to overcome in order to achieve occupation such measures offer no utility, or much less utility, to potential attackers.

It becomes clear that in so far as its value as an instrument of dissuasion is concerned, the argument for non-military defence rests to a very large degree on the plausibility of the case for civilian defence as 'occupation defence.'

However, it should again be pointed out that the military defensive measures which small industrialised countries could effectively take against the types of attack noted above (nuclear attack, bombing, etc.) are extremely limited and that they are practically worthless for the defence and protection of lives and social institutions.

Civilian defence proponents have had relatively little to say about general policies for conflict prevention and the reduction of international tensions. This is related to the conception of civilian defence as an alternative to military defence, fulfilling the same functions; indeed this has meant an explicit turning away from previous proposals by the peace movement such as world government, international peace brigades, etc. This is also related to the 'tough-mindedness' of recent writings since many of the specific proposals of the peace movement were articulations of faith rather than programmes which were likely to be politically implemented. In those relatively few cases where the proponents of civilian defence have made prescriptions which transcend the argument about non-violence as an alternative to the military, these have not generally been very thoroughly worked through. One proposal which is frequently encountered is that the resources which are liberated by the abolition of the military should be used to expand foreign aid programmes substantially; one reason being that the unequal distribution of wealth in the world is an important cause of conflicts. As a humanitarian concern this is a worthwhile idea, but it is far from certain that conflicts would not be more frequent in a world where inequality was less – at least if by conflict one means the overt use of violence.

The fact that objections might be raised to specific proposals which have been made in the past does not, of course, mean that an internationalist rather than a nationalistic perspective is not valuable. Indeed it can be argued that in the smaller nations where security is dependent less on national defence efforts – whether civilian or military – than on developments in the international system in general, an international perspective attempting to cope with the roots of conflicts rather than participating in them or attempting to guard the nation against them is a necessity. Concentration on an analysis of international conflicts which is undistorted by consideration of the short term needs of national defence, of narrow strategic and economic interests and so forth could be an extremely useful role for a small nation to play.

2. DISSUASION

The dissuasion dimension of civilian defence is dependent to a large degree on the perceived efficacy of 'internal defence', that is to say on the perceived efficacy of strategies for non-violent resistance to invasion. Furthermore, in the case of civilian defence the effectiveness of dissuasion is more dependent upon the precise aims of an attack than is military deterrence. Civilian defence methods can do little to prevent an attacker from establishing bases in isolated regions, but they would be much more effective in preventing a change in the political, social and doctrinal structure of the occupied territory.

WAR WITHOUT WEAPONS

a) Deterrence

Broadly speaking, the dissuading effect of civilian defence should arise from a reduction of the potential benefits to be derived by the invader rather than from increasing his costs. With civilian defence 'deterrence' will in general be less potent than it is with military defence but the costs of failing to deter effectively are correspondingly far lower. Nuclear deterrence, the 'balance of terror', is assumed to work because it would be irrational for one nuclear power to attack another using nuclear weapons since the costs to both sides would far exceed any conceivable gains. However, because the use of nuclear weapons is in this way self-defeating, the threat to use such force — which constitutes the nuclear deterrent — loses much of its credibility when made by rational men. For this reason nuclear deterrence presupposes the flawless rationality of the opponent but at the same time it presupposes that the opponent perceives oneself as being not fully rational.

The concept of rationality used in deterrence theory has been increasingly criticised as far too simplistic. Raser (1966) surveying the literature on deterrence theory, notes that: 'decision makers are *not* merely rational calculators of utilities but are men acting under a whole series of constraints' including public opinion, the personality structures of opinion makers, institutional factors (affecting the amount and nature of information they receive and the types of decision they can implement). their ideological predispositions which affect their perception and their interpretation of information received and finally 'the behaviour of other nations will create different kinds of "expectancy states" within the decision makers and these will act as perceptual filters and lenses affecting perceptions and thus decisions.'

Furthermore, 'The conviction is growing that deterrence is only meaningful during crisis situations. During periods of low tension and hostility and low provocation there may be no intent to attack'. (*Ibid.*) It is under crisis conditions that it becomes necessary to deter, yet it is precisely under these conditions which are characterised by extremely high tension, a short time in which to solve crucial problems, anger, low expectations for peaceful solutions and high threats to national goals. In other words precisely when rationality is most needed, irrationality in decision making is most likely. These conclusions are supported by many studies of decision-making under crisis conditions.

Civilian defence has its own dissuasion arguments which also necessarily make similar assumptions about the rationality of decision makers in weighing up the costs and benefits of attack. These arguments are open to the same criticisms as those made above. Nevertheless, in the case of non-military means there is no element of fear involved in the opponent's calculations, less of a crisis situation and no need for the opponent to strike first in order to economise his own forces. For this reason it is more likely that the attacker will actually make the cool, rational calculations of costs and benefits which the reasoning presupposes. Furthermore, as already noted, the consequences of errors, while highly undesirable, are not catastrophic in the same absolute sense as they are in the nuclear case.

The crudities of the 'massive retaliation' theories of the Dulles era have been replaced as strategists and decision makers realised that nuclear threats were simply not a credible response to deter 'low level' hostilities such as minor border clashes, guerilla wars in peripheral areas, etc. However, with many of the proposed flexible responses there is the inherent danger of escalation up to and past the nuclear threshold. One of the major advantages of civilian defence strategies is that they do not invite escalation to progressively more advanced weaponry to the same extent. Needless to say, civilian defence raises many other problems, some of which have been dealt with in this work.

b) Cost of Invasion

There are important parallels between the defence system of a country like Sweden which is not bound to any alliance and civilian defence system like that considered here. In both cases there is no potential for aggression and no potential for retaliation after an attack either. A realistic assessment of the international political and military situation shows that in neither case can the nation defend itself against a major attack (contrast the speculations of U.S. strategists like Herman Kahn on the ability of the U.S. to withstand an all-out Soviet attack) and in both cases the deterrence system is based on the denial of important benefits from attack rather than on inflating the costs.

WAR WITHOUT WEAPONS

In both cases finally, the defence of a small nation against militarily more powerful opponents is the main focus of concern. Thus defence against occupation is taken seriously in contrast, say, to the U.S.A. where no strategists seriously envisage the possibility of occupation or surrender and where to even talk in such terms is perceived as 'defeatist'.

In a discussion of Swedish defence policy (Moberg, 1967) classifies the costs which accrue to an attacker as either 'direct' or 'indirect'. In other words he distinguishes between costs inflicted on the attacker by Swedish defence measures and those inflicted on him in some other way (Moberg, 1967). In civilian defence there are no easily calculable direct costs to the opponent in the sense in which Moberg uses the term, i.e. 'costs that are associated directly with the *war* actions resulting from military attack' *(Ibid.)* Rather the aim of 'deterrence' is to convince the opponent that civilian defence strategies of denial (of cooperation, access to resources, etc.) will *minimise direct benefits* and *maximise indirect costs.*

As with all dissuasion arguments, the opponent is assumed to be 'rational' and to calculate the benefits and costs (direct and indirect) of attack. Given a nation with a well organised and articulated civilian defence policy Galtung suggests that such a calculation might be as follows:

We can gain territorial control over that nation with no difficulty, as quickly as our forces move in. There will be no military counter-activity to control and should there be some sporadic outbursts the defenders are not able to control, we would easily be able to do so. We can establish bases with no difficulty. But their own facilities cannot be used for our purposes, the local population will not be cooperative, there is no sign of internal dissent, which can be used for our purpose they will reject our goods – economic, social, cultural and political – with their non-cooperation. We can ignore that and stick to the bases, but if we do not we are likely to get a millstone around our necks. Of course, we can try to bomb them into submission, but we will then expose ourselves to criticism and dissent from within and without. (1967)

'Indirect costs' are sometimes referred to as 'political costs and cover a wide variety of phenomena. The civilian defence literature has put much emphasis on the indirect costs which derive from

134

the negative evaluation of invasion by other non-involved nations. This may take the form of diminished political support (e.g. the U.S. as a result of the war in Vietnam), of sanctions (such as were applied against Italy after her attack on Ethiopia), or other collective international measures (such as the U.N. response to the Anglo-French Suez expedition in 1956) or, finally, of direct military intervention. Other indirect costs will include weakening the opponent's military capacity by tying down forces which might be needed elsewhere and the possible creation of dissent within the opponent's ranks both in the occupation forces and in the population at home.

It seems clear that civilian defence can offer little or no real resistance to what might be called 'geo-strategic invasion', that is to say an invasion which has the limited objective of securing a strategic territorial position. On the other hand this may be of decreasing importance because bases and strategic positions are becoming decreasingly useful as weapons carriers increase in speed and range and as even 'conventional' military forces are achieving a greater radius of action and are becoming less dependent upon bases. Moreover, the importance of bases is decreasing with their increasing vulnerability.

It is clear nevertheless that strategically motivated invasion remains a possibility and that there is little that civilian defence can do to reduce the immediate benefits of invasion in this case, though most of the points relating to indirect costs still apply.

For a small country faced with a powerful opponent. there is however, also very little a military defence system can do to reduce the possible benefits from invasion or to increase the direct costs. In this case too it is the *indirect costs* which appear to be the most important.

It can reasonably be claimed that it is perhaps not so much the nuclear threat as such, as the general fear of upsetting the political status quo, and the unpredictable consequences this would have which cause the powers in Europe to act with caution and restraint. A nation implementing a civilian defence dissuasion strategy would emphasise such political consequences and this might in some cases play an important role in persuading the opponent of the possible indirect costs of invasions.

The difficulty with arguing in abstract terms about possible civilian defence 'deterrence' strategies, is that the potential costs and benefits to an opponent contemplating invasion vary not only with the defence capability (whether military or non-military) of the defending nation, but also, more importantly, with the objectives of the opponent. For a military defence this is less true (first of all because the tasks of the defence are traditionally defined as those which a military defence has a possibility of carrying out).

The possible range of objectives for invasion with subsequent occupation includes a number of possibilities: the exploitation of raw materials and labour, the establishment of an economic or market system, the imposition of an ideology or political system, intervention in domestic conflict or pre-emptive invasion. Galtung (1967) notes that there are increasingly other, and more sophisticated, ways of achieving these objectives without resort to invasion and occupation. In fact it can be argued that much of the recent history of the relationships between developed and underdeveloped nations may be seen in these terms; the export of ideologies, the exploitation of raw materials and labour, the imposition of political systems are all being achieved, on the whole without invasion and occupation by the West. The relationships between the U.S.S.R. and Eastern European nations may be seen in similar terms with the invasions of Hungary (1956) and Czechoslovakia (1968) as examples where the more sophisticated methods had failed.

c) Achievement of Credibility

Deterrence and dissuasion, whether military or non-military, presuppose that the opponent perceives and evaluates the consequences of attack. This means that not only must there be a defence *capability* but it must also be credible that the defence system will actually be used if required. That is to say, that this capability must be communicated to the opponent and it must have a sufficient credibility.

One immediately encounters a difficulty which — although in a somewhat different form — also applies to military deterrence. To the opponent, the means which the defence intends to use must seem powerful enough to be effective, but in practice this is partly contradictory to the needs of credibility. For even though powerful means may be effective if used, they will often require such sacrifices by the population that the

EXTERNAL DEFENCE: DETERRENCE AND DISSUASION
threat of their being used will have low credibility. The fact that in military defence there is not the same need to take extensive account of popular support is an advantage, seen from this angle.

Several suggestions for increasing the credibility of civilian defence dissuasion have been made. Galtung (1967) and Roberts (1967c), for example, suggest holding civilian defence 'exercises' and ·manoeuvres with a maximum of publicity and with international observers present'. Gleditsch (1965a) suggests communicating the idea of an 'automatic' civilian defence response to invasion arguing that 'the essence of credibility is to commit yourself'. The idea of commitment is also evident in various forms of legislation which have been proposed to prevent collaboration (Porsholt, 1965) and in the proposals to organise civilian defence command structures so that surrender becomes virtually impossible (Gleditsch, 1965a).

Gleditsch, (1965a) also notes that there are some nations – he instances Switzerland – which have a 'natural deterrent' capability – in this case the tunnels through the Alps. In the last war the St. Gotthard and Simplon were of considerable strategic importance to the axis powers but the Swiss were able to make a credible threat that the tunnels would be destroyed if the Germans attempted to occupy the country. This, according to most commentators, served as a major deterrent at several points during the war.

In the case of Denmark the only possible analogy is the straits connecting the Baltic to the North Sea and one might think of an analogous Danish policy of mining the straits in case of occupation. Apart from those objections one may raise on moral grounds (mining the straits could not really be called a non-violent strategy) there are, however, important differences in these two cases. In case of war between East and West the Danish straits would connect enemies, not allies, as did the Swiss tunnels during World War II. Partly for this reason the importance of the straits in wartime – if any – is for military rather than commercial transport. They would therefore become a zone of military offensive and counter-offensive and the front-line would go through them if the confrontation took such a form that passage were genuinely important. A similar situation did not arise for Switzerland.

In peacetime, when the straits are kept open for all transport by virtue of international agreements, the situation is rather different. Here the commercial interest to both East and West in keeping the straits open is considerable, even if not vital. For the U.S.S.R. on the other hand, the interest in keeping the straits open for military convoys in peacetime could aptly be described as vital, since without it the Baltic fleet and the considerable docking and servicing installations situated on the Baltic would be of no avail.

While this is certainly a topic which would deserve closer examination, we may tentatively conclude that a credible Danish threat to sabotage the passage through the straits would have little effect in case of a major war between East and West and might even precipitate Denmark's involvement in the hostilities but that the same threat might well be a potent element in dissuading an isolated attack on Denmark. This would seem to apply whether the attack were anticipated to come from the Eastern or the Western powers.

d) Conclusion

Three aspects of 'external defence' for a civilian defence policy have been considered and compared briefly with their military counterparts. From this the following tentative conclusions have been drawn: civilian defence as the sole means of national defence is highly suitable for allaying fears of aggressiveness and in this sense reducing international tension and dispelling some of the causes and precipitants of war. It provides a 'deterrent' which is much less potent than that of conventional nuclear retaliation strategies, at least if the latter can be made credible. Civilian defence is less effective in two ways: (a) it can only deter under certain sets of assumptions about the war aims of the opponent, and (b) the costs imposed are much lower than those involved in nuclear retaliation. At the same time the consequences of civilian defence deterrence failing are not so catastrophic.

The credibility of civilian defence deterrence raises serious problems. The difficulty here is compounded by lack of past experience on the basis of which to estimate the effectiveness of non-military methods. What little literature exists on the deterrent effects of a civilian defence policy has concentrated on communicating the capability to minimise direct benefits to a would-be invader; it is suggested that another, perhaps more fruitful approach might be to pinpoint and communicate possible or probable *indirect costs.* This would require a fuller examination of some of the more questionable assumptions in current strategic thinking such as the existence of 'balances' of power and terror because it necessarily involves a re-consideration of the very sources of international stability. Finally it has been pointed out that for small countries with large neighbours security is largely independent of *any* defence measures the country may implement. This applies whether or not it is a military defence policy since capabilities must at any rate remain limited, and whether it is a policy of non-alliance or of collective security, since the likelihood of assistance from other nations in case of need is presumably rather more dependent on their actual interests than on formal alliance relationships. For countries in this situation basic research into international conflict might prove to be more rewarding in the long term than research specifically oriented to considerations of their own narrow security goals.

It must finally be strongly emphasised that the post-war tendency to consider defence and security policies in terms of 'deterrence' is a narrowing down of the issue which should not be accepted uncritically. It involves a whole range of entirely gratuitous assumptions, such as the assumption of the 'aggressiveness' of certain countries, or, which ultimately amounts to the same thing, the circular assumption that countries have a natural tendency to 'fill' any 'power vacuum' that has arisen. In such assumptions the conclusion is already implicit that, ultimately, a military solution alone is effective. If one starts by assuming that the political goals of other nations are given *a priori,* are unaffected by the policies of their neighbours and are consistently hostile, then one has not *demonstrated* the need for a military defence and the necessity of deterrence – one has only *assumed* it.

The real problem is of course not to deter an opponent from attacking but more generally to *reduce the likelihood* of military attack or other forms of external pressure, and it is only by comparing the different defence options in this wider perspective that anything can be demonstrated. To do this each particular situation must be considered in its political, strategic and historical context and in this case it cannot be presumed that civilian defence would be unable to compete with traditional military defence.

CHAPTER IX

Combining Civilian and Military Defence

While the official interest which has been shown in the adoption
of civilian defence has been concerned with its use as a part of a
'total defence' concept, i.e. as a *supplement* to military means, the
advocates of civilian defence have been primarily concerned with
its use as the sole means of defence, i.e. as an *alternative* to
military defence.

The problems of 'transarmament' from military to civilian
defence have been considered by many authors (Lakey, 1964;
Roberts, 1967c; *Vereinigung Deutscher Wissenschaftler,* 1967
and others). These deal with a situation where military and
non-military means co-exist, but see this only as a transitional
period until the military component of the defence has been
completely dismantled. Roberts (1967c) and Galtung (1967)
briefly discuss the utility of a combination of the two as a
permanent solution and point out some of the advantages and
drawbacks of this.

The proposals most frequently found, especially among those
strategists and military historians who have shown interest in
this area, is to use military defence as a 'frontier defence' and
let civilian defence take over if and when the frontier defence is
defeated, i.e. after the nation has been occupied.

In the very first analysis it might appear that a combination
of two means of defence is bound to be preferable to either in
isolation — preferable, that is, in the sense of providing more
effective deterrence and a greater likelihood of successful resistance should this be required. On closer examination, however,
the situation is not so simple.

To discuss the relative merits of the 'pure' strategies (either military or non-military) and a combination of them let us ignore for a moment those doubts that can be raised regarding the effectiveness of military and non-military means and simply accept at their face value the arguments which are put forward by the advocates of either of these means.

It is at once evident that in the case of a combination, any expansion of one of the pure defence systems is at the expense of the other if the total resources available for defence are fixed, but this is of relatively little interest in the present context. What we want to consider is the possibility that one of these defence systems itself jeopardises the presumed effectiveness of the other.

Consider first the effect of a civilian defence component being added to a military defence system. For the actual conduct of military operations in case of war, it is hard to see that the simultaneous use of civilian defence could in any way reduce the effectiveness of the military effort. In fact this is merely the 'total defence' concept mentioned above, where the civilian effort is subordinated to the military aims and is ultimately little more than a supporting operation for the military with a view to harrassing further the enemy within the territory he has occupied. Similarly, the fact of retaining an ability for civilian defence and using it after the collapse of the military cannot, it seems, make the military defence either more or less effective.

The situation is much more complicated if we consider the effect of a civilian option upon the ability of the military forces to *deter* a potential aggressor. The ability to use civilian methods alone or as a 'second line of defence' provides an additional physical capability to repel attack and thus strengthens overall deterrence, but by the same token it reduces the *credibility* of the military part of the deterrent, because it increases the likelihood that if it came to it, the military means would not be used at all in the defence. At least this is so if one takes for granted the conventional type of reasoning in the deterrence literature: to deter effectively a state must give the impression that it will definitely retaliate upon attack because each of its other options is less tempting. In those terms it is a weakness to leave oneself an option (occupation defence) which is intermediate between maximum retaliation and surrender. This is all the more important because it is hard to imagine a situation in which a country which is attacked by a nuclear power and which has to choose between surrender, retaliation or non-violent resistance would not opt for the latter course. The more strongly the attacked nation believes in the effectiveness of its *civilian* defence the less effective would be the *deterrence credibility* of its *military* forces.

This is the reason for the taboos on open discussion of policies which imply that retaliation may not in fact be used if it came to it. As Galtung puts it: 'to study the effects of occupation for instance, is tantamount to accepting occupation as a possibility, which then is translated into accepting occupation by cultural alchemy' (1962). An example is provided by the violent congressional reaction to the publication of the report by the Rand Corporation on 'Strategic Surrender' (King, 1967).

Evidently, the lack of alternatives to retaliation and surrender which is a source of strength in conventional deterrence thinking is a catastrophic liability if war should come, but that is not the issue at this point.

On the other hand there is reason to point out that there is a difference between a deterrence strategy based on one's own retaliatory forces and one that relies upon somebody else's nuclear umbrella. Strictly speaking, the above argument is convincing only in the former case, i.e. it only applies fully to the two superpowers. For countries which, like the European NATO members, rely upon the retaliatory capability of allies, the credibility of deterrence is not decisively affected by whether the government has a wider or narrower range of options. What matters in deterrence are not the options of the European governments but those of the American government and whether the latter, if a civilian defence were provided for, would be more ready to let this or that European country manage on its own if attacked (or would get a better pretext for not honouring its commitments). Even if it had been possible for the United States to decide singlehandedly whether, in case of attack, some European country was or was not to use its civilian defence option, one would still have to assume that the arguments which would make that European country prefer a non-military response would not carry the same weight with the American government. We shall not pursue this analysis further because — as with so much of the deterrence reasoning — one soon reaches the level of utter sophistry.

For an alliance-free country without nuclear weapons the situation is somewhat different. There 'deterrence' consists not in reprisals but in the ability to frustrate the opponent of the assumed benefits of occupation. Under those conditions there are only advantages to be derived from adding a non-violent component to the military defence system, although, as we shall see, those advantages are very limited, and the 'mixture' very dangerous for the civilian population. This is undoubtedly an important reason why Sweden, for instance, has shown so much interest in non-violent and civilian means of resistance in comparison with Denmark which, instead, has put the emphasis on para-military forces (the Home Guard).

If one considers realistically what might happen in case one of the major powers were to attack a small NATO member it seems clear that the non-military defence option is worth having in reserve. (As stated above, we here ignore the question of its intrinsic effectiveness). In Schelling's words, such an option 'converts what would have been an assymetry of force into a two-sided bargaining situation' (1967). In fact the histories of many occupations — especially those during World War II — suggest that the population of occupied countries — and particularly those who occupy key administrative positions — lack *any* clear idea of what the appropriate behaviour towards the opponent should be. '. . . in German occupied territories during World War II, patriotic civil servants never knew when to resist and when to cooperate with the Germans to prevent the worst.' (Ebert, 1967). This lack of clear guidelines led to a far from optimal combination of collaboration (often with the best of motives) and resistance, and denied the resistance any real effectiveness, while at the same time exposing the population unnecessarily.

Turning now to a consideration of the possible detrimental effects upon the effectiveness of civilian defence policy which the silmultaneous possession or use of a military defence would have, the situation is much more clear-cut. Most of the arguments for civilian defence lose their validity in this case and it does not seem that any argument can be put forward to suggest that civilian defence would be more effective if a military defence component were added to it.

143

The argument that civilian defence allays the possible fears of the opponent and thus effectively disposes of the danger of pre-emptive attack is of course not longer valid if military means are retained. The moral advantage of having the opponent clearly identified as the aggressor would also be lost because it would always be possible to raise arguments about who provoked or initiated hostilities. For the same reason the unity of the resistance might be much more difficult to achieve.

If military forces are used as a first line of defence and the civilian defence is only set in action afterwards, then the civilian phase in the defence would start off with the psychological disadvantage of knowing that a defeat has already been suffered and, furthermore, with the population conditioned to perceiving the situation in entirely inadequate terms, for instance as a question of frontier defence rather than occupation defence. The opponent's inhibitions as regards the use of violence would have been undermined by the previous use of violence on both sides and it might be much more difficult to prevent small groups among the defenders from using violence themselves. Positive influence techniques would become less potent or virtually useless as a result of the polarisation which is a concomitant of the previous military confrontation.

There are many different ways in which military and non-military means could be combined in the defence of a nation and in fact the argument against mixing the two is not equally strong in all the cases one can think of.

First there is the possibility of using the two defences in clearly differentiated situations, the most obvious being to use military means alone against external aggression (occupation and border violations), and non-violent means only against internal aggression, such as military coups. From the point of view of this present discussion this combination does not seem to give rise to any objections — but then it is also not a case of civilian defence.

Another possibility is to use the two approaches in different geographical areas. If these are clearly separated the objections raised above would again be less valid. Many instances can be found in history where areas could not be properly defended by military means and where a social defence was more or less consciously adopted instead. The clearest example is provided by the World War II plans for the defence of Switzerland against a German attack: In case of attack the plains in the North would be immediately evacuated and the armed forces would retire to a *réduit* in the Alps which could be effectively defended. Extensive preparations were made for non-cooperation in the North, including the sabotage of much of the industry. (Rather evidently, it is not normally possible to generalise this approach and defend bases only by military means while using civilian defence for the rest of the country, since most bases cannot be defended without their hinterland).

The last possibility is to use both means simultaneously and more or less closely co-ordinated. This may either take the form of a 'total defence' with a clear subordination of civilian efforts to military needs, or else it might take the form of partly violent resistance (civil insurrection, partisan or guerrilla war). For small industrialised countries faced with attack by one of the larger powers both of these possibilities seem to be completely pointless militarily, while at the same time exposing the population to a serious risk of reprisals.

The best-known proposal for a mixed military/civilian defence is probably that of George F. Kennan, which is worth quoting at some length:

If the armed forces of the United States and Britain were not present on the Continent, the problem of defense for the continental nations would be primarily one of the internal health and discipline of the respective national societies, and of the manner in which they were organized to prevent the conquest and subjugation of their national life by unscrupulous and foreign-inspired minorities in their midst. What they need is a strategic doctrine addressed to this reality. Under such a doctrine, armed forces would indeed be needed, but I would suggest that as a general rule these forces might better be para-military ones, of a territorial-militia type, somewhat on the Swiss example, rather than regular military units on the pattern of the Second World War. Their functions should be primarily internal rather than external. It is on the front of political realities, not on regular military battlefields, that the threat of Russian Communism must primarily be met. The training of such forces ought to be such as to prepare them not only to offer whatever overt resistance might be possible to a foreign invader, but also to constitute the core of a civil resistance movement on any territory that might be overrun by the enemy. . .

. . . the primary purpose of the dispositions would be not the defense of the country at the frontier, though naturally one would aim to do whatever could be done in this respect, but rather its defense at every village crossroads. The purpose would be to place the country in a position where it could face the Kremlin and say to it: "Look here, you may be able to overrun us, if you are unwise enough to attempt it, but you will have small profit from it; we are in a position to assure that not a single Communist or other person likely to perform your political business will become available to you for this purpose; you will find here no adequate nucleus of a puppet regime; on the contrary, you will be faced with the united and organized hostility of an entire nation; your stay among us will not be a happy one; we will make you pay bitterly for every day of it; and it will be without favourable longterm political prospects.

I think I can give personal assurance that any country which is in a position to say this to Moscow, not in so many words, but in that language of military posture and political behaviour which the Russian Communists understand best of all, will have little need of foreign garrisons to assure its immunity from Soviet attack. (Kennan, 1958)

It is at once apparent that this strategic doctrine rests on the idea of the social and internal character of the defence and ultimately on the concept of popular or civilian resistance. Once this is admitted, however, it becomes difficult to see any reason but the force of tradition why Kennan should retain the notion of a military or violent component to the defence. The ability of the military forces to operate effectively is seriously affected by the initial assumption that the opponent can occupy the most important strategic positions in the country and that moreover the military forces are tied to the territory so that they are poorly equipped to pursue the opponent into his own territory. Under such circumstances the contribution of the violent defence to the weakening of the attacker would be slight. It is therefore no wonder that in his imagined address to the Kremlin, Kennan makes no reference whatsoever to the effects of the military effort but relies entirely on the effectiveness of non-violent means. The violent part of Kennan's strategic doctrine therefore seems practically useless from a defence point of view while subjecting civilians to an utterly unnecessary risk of reprisals.

CHAPTER X

Non-Violent Defence in Classical Strategic Theory

It has been noted on several occasions that nowhere in the literature on non-violent defence does one find anything remotely like a strategic analysis of the confrontation which results when military occupation is countered by non-violent resistance. One does find a number of scattered suggestions which are often pertinent but which, not being placed in the framework of a strategy, do not show their *necessary* character but appear as so many 'useful ideas' or 'naive proposals' depending on one's point of view. What one finds in the literature are really collections of 'tactics', of methods for putting pressure on the opponent. But from these no strategy can ever emerge. It is impossible to start with the methods of Chapter II and with them construct a strategy. One must start with a strategy and then determine the role — large or small — of each tactical method in relation to it. The result of applying a system of forces haphazardly to a body is normally that they cancel each other out. To be effective, pressures must be given a common point of application and a common direction. The task of strategy is precisely to provide an overall view of the entire confrontation, to offer criteria for distinguishing useful from less useful means, and criteria for organising these means into a coherent and purposeful whole.

The lack of a general strategic conception is undoubtedly the gravest single shortcoming in the literature on non-violence. It shares this shortcoming with current military defence thinking. Like much work on civilian defence, military defence thinking does not derive from a strategy, but consists rather of collections of military means of pressure, the cumulated effect of which is simply assumed to add up to a defence policy. This lack of an overall strategic analysis on both sides of the fence is the main factor which precludes a meaningful dialogue between the proponents of either, and — for the same reasons — prevents a 'pragmatic' comparison of these two modes of defence. As long as the general features of a strategy are not made explicit, any claims about the superiority of either mode of defence must remain pure conjecture.

The purpose of this chapter is to sketch what a strategy of non-violent defence would necessarily have to be, thereby situating this mode of defence in relation to other possible approaches. In so doing we base ourselves on classical strategic theory as developed by von Clausewitz. This theory makes two main assumptions: first, that the aim of war is to 'win' over the opponent, so that the conflict is conceived of as pure antagonism; second, that winning is the sole criterion by which possible courses of action are to be judged. The theory is therefore directly applicable to the 'negative' and 'pragmatic' approaches to non-violence followed in this book and in most of the recent literature. With a 'positive' perspective on conflict, or if the case for non-violence is argued on ethical grounds, classical strategic theory would be of no relevance.

Strategic theory seeks to determine which plans of action (strategies) are most likely to lead to victory over the enemy. It does not stop to consider costs and does not seek to minimise the human or material losses incurred in the process. 'Philanthropy', Clausewitz says, 'must be extirpated' before one can embark on the strategic analysis of war. In that sense war may be compared with a game of chess where the one and only aim is to checkmate the king. How many pawns are lost in the process is of no interest whatsoever, except in so far as it affects the prospects of a successful checkmate. So in the strategy of war: soldiers and civilians have no value *per se*. Either they are strategic resources (or in some way affect these), or else they are worthless and their loss irrelevant.

Nevertheless strategic analysis is not immoral but amoral. The determination of 'best' strategies (in terms of securing victory) is a purely intellectual task. Death and destruction result from the application of strategy to war, and it is here that ethical considerations can and must enter. It is often the case in a struggle that the preferred strategy (meaning desirable and acceptable in terms of costs) is not the 'best' one (in the above sense). Overriding considerations may thus rule out certain strategies which would have provided a greater likelihood of success, and make one settle for less. The *im*morality (and logical confusion) of the apologists of *Realpolitik* is precisely to be found in their failure to make this distinction between the strategically optimal and the morally desirable. In identifying these two concepts they make two assumptions which are generally true in the case of parlour games, but which are always wrong in war: namely that there is a perfect polar relationship between the 'players' so that each must pursue exclusively his own interest and, secondly, that the pursuit of 'victory' is a full and adequate measure of that interest.

Classical strategic theory is almost entirely the work of von Clausewitz, and is to be found fully developed in his major work *On War* , in which it is applied (mainly) to the Napoleonic wars. The same theoretical frame has been used by Mao Tse-Tung (in *On Protracted War*) to analyse guerrilla warfare in China. The theoretical differences between these authors are hardly more than questions of emphasis. A third source which has been made use of is Glucksmann's *The Discourse of War* which provides a more transparent formulation of the theoretical principles than does Clausewitz himself. In addition it gives an analysis of nuclear weapons in Clausewitzian theory on which we have drawn extensively.

None of these authors, of course, deal with non-violence (except perhaps von Clausewitz, a few of whose remarks can possibly be interpreted as contemptuous rejections of it), but that does not matter. Clausewitzian theory is not a set of dogmatic rules of more or less universal validity, but a *method* for analysing a confrontation and for discerning effective strategies from less effective ones. It is therefore in any case necessary to reapply the theory from first principles each time a new conflict is to be analysed. Although he has often been read that way, Clausewitz' purpose never was to affirm that cavalry are better placed behind than in line with infantry, but to expose the methods by which the best deployment can be determined in each particular case.

At first sight it might appear that the best approach to develop a strategy is as follows: first decide what is really worth defending and what is not, what the enemy might want to conquer, and how, considering the situation from his point of view, he is likely to go about it (i.e.,draw up 'scenarios' of the possible attacks you may be subjected to). Then survey available or potential means of defence deleting those (if any) which are morally unacceptable, and decide how to deploy them to counter each attack scenario. Assuming such a plan of deployment were implemented, find out what would then appear to be the best attack scenarios from the enemy's point of view (i.e., find the flaws in the defences). If these differ from the original scenarios repeat the whole procedure with the new ones, and go on in this way until no further improvement in the defences seems possible.

Despite the fact that this 'stop-gap' procedure is the method by which military planners normally proceed, this approach to the problem is a complete mistake and the surest path to disaster. It violates virtually all of the basic principles of strategy. To show this, and to indicate how to approach the problem correctly, it will be necessary to expose the principal features of classical strategic theory before turning to non-violent defence as such, and to the application of strategy to the particular conditions of the day.

1. CLAUSEWITZIAN STRATEGIC THEORY

The main elements of the theory which need to be considered are the relations between war and politics, the principle of polarity or unchecked escalation in war, the principle of the superiority of the defence over the offence, and the concept of centre of gravity.

First it is necessary to distinguish two concepts which we call the *aim* of war and the *purpose* of war: the former is military and the latter political. This distinction is the key to Clausewitz' theory of strategy, indeed to any unified strategy of war at all. Politics sets the purpose. In a very general sense it is 'to gain possession of something' and it differs from war to war. When politics resorts to war the political purpose is temporarily replaced – displaced in fact – by the *aim* of war, which is to achieve victory, 'to subdue the enemy', to 'force him to comply with our will'. Thus the *aim* of warfare is always the same but the *purpose* of warfare is usually a different one for each war (and different for the two belligerents). Therefore, victory on the one hand, and

151

the fruits of victory or their enjoyment on the other are not to be confused.

This displacement of the purpose by the aim is the leading idea. Through it, each war becomes an indivisible whole, and its different elements (battles and campaigns) become organised in relation to a single strategic target (the aim: victory) which becomes the only standard by which they are to be measured. What would otherwise merely be blind actions thus become strategic moves. Furthermore this displacement ensures the theoretical unity of war: it makes a unified theory possible since all wars have the same aim. Finally the displacement of the *purpose* by the *aim* determines the principal characteristics of war: it becomes a pure struggle of polar opposites which necessarily tends to escalate to the extreme, to the full and immediate use of all the mobilisable forces. In a political confrontation where all sorts of purposes may enter, there may be a certain community of interests, compromises and trade-offs are then possible and there can be no complete polarity. In war the aims are completely antagonistic; one belligerent can only win to the extent that the other loses. The struggle is an absolute and uncompromising contest for ascendancy: 'every advantage gained on the one side is a corresponding disadvantage on the other.' No limitation in the amount of force used is possible; no pause is conceivable, for if one belligerent wishes to delay action, for instance to restore his forces, to that same extent and for that same reason the other must wish to precipitate it.

Such, in crudest theory, is war. In reality it is very different: 'If', as Clausewitz says, 'we cast a glance at military history in general, we find . . . that standing still and doing nothing is quite plainly the normal condition of an Army in the midst of war, acting, the exception.' In each particular case all sorts of factors may cause a standstill: the timidity of commanders and cabinets, overestimation of the enemy forces must accelerate war beyond its natural tendency. To explain the theoretical paradox that war is often slow, inconclusive and timid when it ought, according to theory, be always quick, decisive and of utmost violence, something else is needed: there must be a general principle at work to which polarity is not applicable and which will 'like a ratchet wheel in machinery, from time to time produce a complete standstill.'

NON-VIOLENT DEFENCE IN STRATEGIC THEORY

Clausewitz then proceeds to show that there is only one such possible ratchet wheel, namely the superiority of the defence over the attack. If A is too weak to attack B and would rather wait, it is in the interest of B to be attacked at once, not later. In this case there is complete polarity, but it does not follow that B is strong enough, himself to attack A. Hence polarity breaks down and pauses in war become logically possible once it is recognized that defence and attack are different things and not of equal strength. In classical strategic theory, therefore, military stalemate, cease-fire and peace are not the result of some delicate balance of opposing strength, of an impossible *equality* of antagonistic forces, but of the *inequality* of the forces of offence and defence. As Glucksmann (1969) has shown, these two principles — of polarity and of the superiority of the defence — together constitute the necessary and sufficient foundations of classical strategic theory. As they interact with the reality of particular nations, their moral and material forces, the weapons of the time, and the accidents of military genius and mediocrity they produce the complex and diverse phenomenon of war as we encounter it in each epoch.

The principle of the superiority of the defence over the offence may at first seem counter-intuitive as it would appear that superior forces must be the decisive factor. But it is so only if we conceive of the confrontation in terms of a battle, army against army, where the forces of each are given in advance. However, the importance of the principle lies precisely in the fact that it deals with the war as a whole. It addresses itself not to what can be done with given force levels but to the size of these force levels throughout the war, to the different types of initiatives the belligerents can and cannot take, and establishes an asymmetry between them — providing a measure of the opposing, forces which is not a mere material counting procedure tank for tank, man for man, but a measure of the real strategic potential of the enemies actual conditions of combat.

How would one prove this principle? Rather: in what sense is it true? It is logically necessary; that follows from what we have already said: without it there could be no pause in war, and, to put it in very crude terms, the system of states as it exists and has existed, could not be stable, and there could only be a single world-wide empire or continuous war. In this sense the principle of the superiority of the defence is already implied by the conception of escalation as the natural form of war.

But then it does not suffice for a theory that its propositions should be logically necessary. They must also have a certain correspondence with reality. Yet it would be of no avail to try to illustrate with examples from particular wars, for the principle does not maintain that it is always (or even mostly) the defence which prevails in war. This principle has to do with the *course* of war, not its outcome, and what it affirms is that the defence decides (or rather has the greater say in deciding) what form the war shall take. (Exactly what this means we shall see later). What we must show is therefore that in war the defence can take certain initiatives, mobilise certain resources, and that the possibilities of the offence are much more limited in this respect.

The best defence, conventional wisdom has it, is offence. What this means is that in war the offence alone can achieve a rapid and final decision. Offence is not 'better defence than defence', but it may render defence unnecessary. The superiority of the defence derives from the fact that where the offence is not immediately successful it soon wears itself down. The defence on the other hand can go on mobilizing resources. In this it has the advantage of combating on its own terrain (information, support, supplies, etc.). Furthermore the thrust of the offence itself, helps mobilisation of resources for the defence by the popular hostility it generates (increased ability to levy taxes, to conscript troops, to turn popular uprising, etc.) and by the envy, jealousy or anxiety it creates in previously neutral states or among its own allies. Thus it is a general principle that if it can hold out for a while, time will work for the defence and give it the strength, not only to hold the offence at bay, but also, increasingly, to counter-attack. The offence must always hope for a quick outcome. It has the advantage of the surprise in the initial attack 'of the whole on the whole', it determines at first where to attack and has the initiative in space, but nonetheless it is forced to attack the strongest points of the defence, and even here, therefore, it is dependent on the previous dispositions of the defence. Moreover, after the initial offensive strike the defence has the initiative in time. It decides when and where to hit back. It therefore determines the structure of the whole war and can do so to suit its own advantage. Unless the war is quickly settled by the victory of the offence it is, in the literal sense, the defence which *conducts* the war. Time being on its side it can choose to attack the weakest points of the enemy first. It does not have to finish him in a quick blow but can wear him down.

The intention here is not to 'prove' the 'truth' of the theoretical principle of the superiority of the defence. Theoretical principles can never be proven by reference to facts. They can be shown to be logically necessary within a theory and to be not in contradiction with the facts, indeed readily reconcileable with them once the theoretical meaning of these principles is properly understood. Their ultimate 'proof' lies in the usefulness in practical application of the theory of which they are part. This, therefore, must be postponed until the other main elements of the theory have been considered.

'The aim of war in conception must always be the overthrow of the enemy; this is the fundamental idea from which we set out.'

Now what is this overthrow? Is it the destruction of the enemy's army, his complete disarmament, or the conquest of his country? Clausewitz puts great emphasis on each of these factors. In his time and in most of history they have indeed been 'the surest commencement, and in all cases the most essential.' Yet he is emphatic that the importance of these factors is not to be elevated into a universally valid dogma:

All that theory can here say is as follows: that the great point is to keep the overruling relations of both parties in view. Out of them a certain centre of gravity, a centre of power and movement, will form itself, on which everything depends; and against this centre of gravity of the enemy, the concentrated blow of all the forces must be directed.

He goes on to illustrate: Alexander had his centre of gravity in his army, so had Gustavus Adolphus, Charles XII, and Frederick the Great, and the career of any one of them would soon have been brought to a close by the destruction of his fighting force; in states torn by internal dissensions, this centre generally lies in the capital, in small states dependent on greater ones, it lies generally in the army of these allies; in a confederacy, it lies in the unity of interests, in a national insurrection, in the person of the chief leader, and in public opinion; against these points the blow must be directed.

To concentrate the blow of all one's forces against the centre

155

of gravity and to attack it 'with the greatest possible dispatch', as Clausewitz says, what does that mean? It is not a prescription for action, not a strategy in itself, but the principle by which strategy is to be measured. Countless delays and roundabout manoeuvres may be justified in war. The principle gives a meaning to the word 'justified'. It states that detours, delays and the diversion of forces to the attack of secondary targets is correct strategy in so far as it adds to one's ability to reach the main target with the maximum force and maximum speed, and is otherwise to be rejected. The correct strategy follows a straight line, but projected on a map that line, to the uninformed, may appear tortuous. It follows that this principle of maximum force and maximum dispatch is inseparable from the principle affirming the existence of the centre of gravity, its role as the focal point of the war, its character of summarising the whole struggle in one point and of being, not only similar in form to the different battles of which the war is composed, but their sole measure and justification.

As the buyer decides which article to purchase, and the seller what it shall cost, so in war it is the offence which decides what the purpose shall be but it is the defence which chooses the centre of gravity. It does not, however, choose this point arbitrarily. As everything else in war, its location is subordinated to reasons of policy (a question to which we return later). What is important to note at this point is that it is essentially by the choice of a mode of *defence* that the centre of gravity is determined.

Consider a specific example: Denmark in 1974, faced – so we assume for the sake of the argument – with a Soviet threat. Two modes of defence are normally considered to be worth contemplating: armed neutrality, and the Atlantic Alliance. In the former case, armed neutrality, the centre of gravity is evidently the Danish armed forces, and it is upon their annihilation that the attack must concentrate. The target, of course, is less the physical strength of these forces than their moral strength and, as in 1940, that of the political authorities. In the second case, that of an alliance with the United States and reliance upon their forces (and, to a lesser degree, those of other Western European powers), the centre of gravity is the solidarity of that alliance. What Clausewitz says in the piece just quoted, that 'in small states dependent on greater ones, [the centre of gravity] lies generally in the army of these allies' is true in many cases (viz. Napoleon's great weakness in his inability to strike at the main allies of the European coalition: Britain and Russia), but it does not apply in this one. The conquest of Denmark evidently does not presuppose the conquest of the United States. If the Soviet purpose (i.e. the political goal) lies in Denmark it would be sheer madness to strike a blow at the American forces. To strike one at the Danish forces would be a waste at best, and counter-productive at worst, as it would probably be the surest way to solidify the alliance. The centre of gravity being the solidarity of the alliance, it is against this point that the forces must be thrown. Military action against Denmark, if indeed any had been advisable, would have to be in the form of carefully dosed stings, meant, not to weaken the Danish forces (as noted this would be pointless or dangerous) but to try to strain the alliance.

These examples should suffice to make the main points clear: first, that there is in each case a specific centre of gravity, and that it is (on the whole) determined by the mode of defence chosen; second, that it is of paramount importance for the attacker to identify this centre of gravity correctly and to aim his blow directly at it; finally, that the centre of gravity determines, among the many different means at the *attacker's* disposal, which ones can be used and must be used (and how to use them) and which ones are useless.

It is now possible to see exactly what is meant by the superiority of the defence over the offence and to understand in what sense it is absolute and inalienable: the defence, by choosing the centre of gravity, also chooses 'where' the attack shall occur, 'what' shall be attacked, and 'how' (with what 'weapons'). Properly used this is an immense and often decisive advantage (cf. how the form of warfare in Vietnam has been entirely determined by what is strategically speaking the defence: the guerrilla forces. Also how this form of warfare makes certain weapons useless, if not worse: those of strategic bombing for instance). It can also be seen that the superiority of the defence is not historically contingent and has nothing whatsoever to do with the peculiarities of the weapons which happen to exist in a given epoch. Nor is there any contradiction between this superiority on the one hand, and on the other, the obvious historical fact that wars have often been won by the attacker. The defence can force the struggle to that point where it itself is strongest, but it does not always do so, and it may be too weak even in that point. Besides, any number of mistakes may be made in the implementation of a defence strategy in practice: in the conduct of war.

The advantage of the theoretical vantage point used here, and the reason why it was necessary to approach the subject of defence strategy the roundabout way taken, now becomes apparent. Given a catalogue (however comprehensive) of 'weapons' and means of defence (however broadly conceived) which are potentially available for a small Western European country, and given another catalogue of 'scenarios', of descriptions of the possible forms a Soviet attack might take, no amount of speculation could ever have shown this central point, namely that it is the *offence* which is the dependent factor and which must mould itself after the defence. On the contrary. with the method of 'scenarios' and counter-measures, it is already built *into the assumptions* that it is the defence which must mould itself after the offence. The reason for such a mistake would be easy to pinpoint: it would have arisen from giving to the concept of defence not its precise strategic meaning, but a vague political one — something like 'protection' — thus assuming that defence consists in protecting whatever happens to be attacked. Anyone who is familiar with chess knows how disastrous such a piece-by-piece strategy would be.

Nor would it of course make any sense to settle priorities first, adding to the other catalogues a third one of 'things thought worth defending'. For in strategy things are worth defending only in proportion as they may serve to defend one's own centre of gravity and attack that of the opponent. Hence their value can be determined only after a strategy has been found, not before.

In fact there are generally two distinct centres of gravity in war. One is determined by the defence and is — or rather should be — the point of attack of the offence in the first place. If that one holds, if the defence succeeds in absorbing and containing the blow of the offence as it reaches its maximum intensity (the 'culminating point' of the war, in Clausewitz' terms) then the counter-attack becomes possible and, as time goes by, increasingly so. While continuing to protect its own centre of gravity against the pressure of the enemy forces, the defence will now also attack the second centre of gravity, that of the forces of the offence when they serve in the defence. It may seem that this second centre of gravity is determined by the offence, just as the first one is by the defence, and that therefore the initial attacker, the offence, must have the upper hand in the counter-offensive. This is however only partly true, for the second centre of gravity largely depends on the means used in the initial attack. Generally, the 'purpose' of the counter-offensive is not an independent political goal, 'to gain possession of something', but the destruction or explusion of the means with which the enemy attacked. But these means themselves are to some extent determined by the choice of the first centre of gravity. Therefore in choosing this first centre of gravity one has a certain influence both over the means which the offence will have to use and, by implication, over the centre of gravity of those forces, the 'Achilles heel' where their strength can be destroyed. This illustrates the intimate relation of mutual determination which exists between offence and defence and between the successive phases in the war. In the discussion of non-violent defence this second centre of gravity will be of considerable importance, but until then it may safely be ignored.

Like the offence, the defence must seek to concentrate all its forces on the centre of gravity. It must do this both when trying to withstand the initial blow of the attacker, and, later, when trying to sustain the defence while the forces needed for the counter-offensive are being built up. One consequence of this is that it is very unlikely, in the midst of war, after the enemy has annihilated the centre of gravity that one could regain one's balance after the blow, choose a new centre of gravity, concentrate new forces upon it, and fall back on it for defence. This was illustrated in Chapter IX where the idea of a two-level defence — first military, then civilian defence — did not appear practicable.

In a very simplified and abstract form, the centre of gravity gives a shorthand representation of the most important basic features of a strategic doctrine, stripped of all the confusing details in which it is necessarily wrapped when it takes its practical, applicable form as a fully deployed system, with all the attendant hardware, organisations, doctrines, role allocations and so forth. This can be illustrated with the two modes of defence considered previously: armed neutrality and the Atlantic Alliance. When they are seen in their theoretically pure form as centres of gravity the general weaknesses of these two modes of defence become readily apparent. In fact it is not easy to think of anything weaker and more vulnerable on which to base a defence than the strength (in its various meanings) of the Danish armed forces or the political cohesion of the Atlantic Alliance. But apart from this, the need to concentrate all the forces of the defence on the centre of gravity immediately shows one fundamental and irreparable shortcoming of these modes of defence. Since in choosing a mode of defence we *ipso facto* choose a centre of gravity, a major consideration must be to so choose the former so that it does indeed become possible to 'pile up' forces in defence of the latter. But both of the alternatives fail to meet even this simple criterion of a good strategy, for both centres of gravity are points on which there is virtually no possibility of concentrating defensive forces. There are very narrow limits to the strength of armed forces Denmark is able to build up (the centre of gravity in the first example), and to improve the solidarity of the alliance (the centre of gravity in the second example) there is probably absolutely nothing Denmark can do. Both modes of defence are, strategically speaking, complete dead-ends, in the sense that with both, all expansion, all strengthening of the defence is excluded. So is, by the same token, virtually all initiative and resourcefulness, particularly with latter of the two. The former, it can be seen, does permit some limited flexibility — revealed in the ambiguity of the concept of the 'strength' of the forces. In their applied form as defence policies implemented in practice, strategies, of course, retain those shortcomings they have in their pure, stripped form as centres of gravity. Only they may be much less apparent, both to oneself and to potential enemies.

A few additional points need to be made before we have all the elements of the theory which are needed to analyse non-violent defence in terms of classical strategic theory. First a remark on the 'choice' of the centre of gravity: to choose a centre of gravity is not to pick arbitrarily on some material or symbolic object and then proclaim that not until that object is conquered or destroyed by the enemy shall we admit defeat. What one chooses is a mode of defence. More or less uniquely this imposes a centre of gravity *objectively* on both belligerents, in the sense that they have no choice but to concentrate their forces on it. This centre of gravity is that point at the heart of the defence which, if it holds out enables the defence to continue the struggle even if weakened, and which, if it falls, must necessarily lead to the collapse of the entire defence, whether for reasons of morale or for material reasons.

But how then are the mode of defence and the corresponding centre of gravity related to the *purpose* of the attacker (i.e. his political goal). Inspired by the idea of non-cooperation in civilian defence one might be tempted to reason as follows: the point in non-cooperation is to deny the enemy his purpose; therefore the mode of defence must consist in perpetuating denial; and therefore the centre of gravity must somehow be the ability to perpetuate denial. This would be a complete mistake. It is so because it fails to take account of the separation of aim and purpose. When war occurs the purpose is displaced by the aim. The entire activity of the enemy (if he acts intelligently) is directed towards the aim (annihilating the centre of gravity), not towards the purpose. Therefore it is not necessarily so that one must seek to bar access to the purpose, and therefore there need not exist any simple relationship of 'protection' between centre of gravity and purpose. The above view would be as false as the idea that in military strategy the defence must somehow be situated 'in front of' the purpose, constituting a kind of physical obstruction. This is obviously false and completely ignores the possibility of a strategic withdrawal, pending counter-attack (strategic withdrawal of Russian forces before Napoleon in 1812, guerrilla strategy of withdrawal, etc.). What really matters is that the centre of gravity should be so chosen that as long as it is preserved intact, counter-offensive and reconquest are possible.

This should suffice to clarify the main points: centre of gravity, its relation to the mode of defence, and to the superiority of the defence over the offence. It remains to explain how war is related to politics.

No other statement by Clausewitz is more widely quoted than the assertion that war is a 'continuation' and an 'instrument' of politics, and none is more often misunderstood. It is not some sort of Bismarckian 'Blood and Iron' philosophy that he gives voice to, neither is it an article of prudent statecraft, or an affirmation of the moral legitimacy of war. It is meant to be a scientific statement about the nature of war.

What it affirms is, first, that war always has a political purpose — war arises out of a social and political context — and, second, that after war has taken over and the aim has displaced the purpose, still it is 'by no means an independent thing, in itself.' When war erupts, its own laws of escalation and uncompromising struggle do not completely take command.

'Our own power, the enemy's power, allies on both sides, the characteristics of the people and their Governments respectively, etc.' are of a political nature and determine the form war takes. The limits of war are still set by policy, which penetrates the entire act of war. Should war, following its natural bent and losing sight of political demands, reach extremities and divorce means from ends, this 'extreme effort would be wrecked by the opposing weight of forces within itself.'

Because of this complete subjection to politics, war does not normally assume its 'absolute form', but remains, in Clausewitz' words, 'a half-and-half thing': 'war [as it actually occurs] may be a thing which is sometimes war [as it appears in theory] in greater, sometimes in a lesser degree.' This gives its meaning that the expression *utmost* use of force in attacking or defending the centre of gravity. There may be no logical limit to the force one may think of using, but there certainly is a political one.

Nonetheless, 'the political [purpose] is no despotic lawgiver. . . it must accommodate itself to the nature of the means'. Where the purpose in war is petty and unimportant, few forces will be put into the offence, few will be needed by the defence, and in any case, few will be forthcoming. Such were the wars of the seventeenth and eighteenth century when social and political conditions severely limited the size of armies, and when, if one was destroyed, a new one was not easily got. No one could afford to accept battle unless certain of victory, and in this fact, political ambitions found their necessary, and political fears their sufficient limitations, and, reflecting the weakness of motives, wars dragged themselves feebly along.

Without a 'grand and powerful purpose' the full mobilization of the forces of the defence is not possible. Certain forms of warfare presuppose certain forms of policy. In proportion to the degree that war attains to its absolute form, its relation to policy therefore becomes tighter and more completely determinate. The more impetuous and self-serving war appears to be, the more completely is it regulated by politics. Never before, Clausewitz maintains, had war been more absolute, and never before had it been more purely political, than it was under the French Revolution and Empire. Mao Tse-Tung makes absolutely the same point when maintaining that only with a revolutionary policy is it possible to conduct the protracted people's war to its end; and, further, that there is no more absolute war than it, and no war which, down to the minutest details, is more completely determined in its form by its political ends. As noted in Chapter III one finds in much of the literature on non-violence a similar idea in the assertion of the necessarily democratic and participatory character of the form and of the goal of civilian defence.

To say that one 'chooses' a mode of defence is therefore a crude over-simplification. The political conditions and the conditions of warfare in a particular epoch determine both the nature and extent of the purpose of war and the means which the offence and the defence can mobilise, but they are also themselves determined by them. Nowhere in the chain is there truly a point where one can say: here is the determinant factor, the rest follows. War and politics, as much as the offence and defence, stand in a complex and intimate relation of mutual determination in which policy must adapt itself to the general conditions of war, as war must to those of policy. But the relation is not a symmetrical one. War is ultimately subordinate to politics, as is the offence to the defence, and this subordination is never more absolute than when war approximates to its pure form.

2. THE UNITY OF THE RESISTANCE

If a country adopts a defence method based on non-violence it *ipso facto* chooses what is to be the centre of gravity of its defence. What is this centre of gravity? In previous chapters it has shown up time and again as being the focus upon which everything has concentrate and the basic resource, the loss of which meant the collapse of the resistance: it is the *unity* of the resistance. It is against this point that the whole thrust of the attack must be directed and to its preservation that all efforts of the defence must tend. To attacker and defender alike, this unity above all else is crucial. It is the only standard by which specific weapons, means and actions can and must be weighed.

Let us consider how the general theoretical principles fare when applied to this particular case. The most important from our point of view is the principle that means, whatever they be – a conventional battle, a piece of artillery, a strike, an act of sabotage — have no intrinsic value whatsoever, except in so far as they relate to the centre of gravity. If they have no bearing upon it they become mere wasteful or counter-productive paraphernalia. This is to be taken in its literal meaning in the form of warfare discussed here. The utility of a rifle is not measured by its ability to shoot but by its ability to destroy the unity of the resistance. If it cannot be used to destroy that unity it is just a piece of iron. If the attacker ignores this he merely makes things more difficult for himself and easier for the resistance. If the attacker loses sight of the fact that the unity of the resistance is the ultimate target, his shots are as likely to cement the resistance together as to break it down.

The invasion of Czechoslovakia provides a forceful illustration of this. The invading armies were taken by surprise by the novel mode of defence used on Czechoslovakia. Their initial belief that once the country had been successfully occupied and armed resistance subdued the main task would be over, was entirely mistaken. Because the centre of gravity had shifted, the act of occupation in itself contributed little or nothing towards achieving the aim, and hence the purpose of the invasion. On the contrary, it was the tanks in the streets of Prague which themselves *created* the unity of the resistance, a unity which had not been there before, or had been so to a much lesser extent, and which completely silenced the orthodox wing in the party, the strengthening of which must surely have been once the invaders' purposes. These tanks were worse than scrap-iron, they were like the grenade which explodes in the hands of the thrower.

Gradually the invading forces learnt the lessons. They brought in *genuinely* useful equipment (such as tracking stations and jamming transmitters); they removed the tanks and most of the troops from the streets (ostensibly as a concession. Perhaps it was felt to be one, but it was certainly in the best interests of the invading forces); and they began the political manoeuvres which alone could succeed. Few events could better illustrate the general principle that in war it is the defence, not as is generally assumed to be the case, the offence, which chooses the weapons, on condition, of course, that it is aware of this prerogative and turns it to advantage. And that is why, as was said at the outset, the method of the military planner who pieces together a defence as a collection of counter-measures to attack 'scenarios' is a complete mistake and the surest path to disaster.

This is not to say that the armed forces of the occupant are completely useless in this kind of warfare. All that is being said is that their usefulness is measured by their effect upon the centre of gravity and by nothing else. This severely curtails their utility. In particular it means that sheer numbers are of little relevance in this context. There are two main ways in which armed forces may be used: one is to terrorise the population. As noted in Chapter V, and as is now almost self-evident, such terrorism must be selective: it must hit specific groups of people to the exclusion of others, seeking in this way to drive a wedge between the groups. Indiscriminate terrorism is most likely to cement the unity of the resistance. But intelligently applied, selective terrorism, it seems, may often be a powerful weapon. It is to be noted, however, that what matters is not to make the resistance less extreme for the sake of it, to frighten it into submission. The occupant may wish to encourage certain groups to a resistance which is more radical than that which others are willing or able to engage in. The second possibility is to use the armed forces to run certain non-military operations such as strike breaking, economic blockading of certain groups, etc. in so far as this is relevant for the war aim. Here they merely serve as a well-disciplined corps. The workers' soup kitchens in the Ruhrkampf are an example, although not a very convincing one.

There are many ways in which the occupant may seek to disrupt the unity of the resistance. The Ruhrkampf and Czechoslovakia provide two quite different examples. In the first case privations, in the long run, affected different groups differently (small shopkeepers and self-employed being particularly hard hit). This, as explained in Chapter VI, was in some measure intentionally exploited by the occupant, and the divisions were consciously fostered — those between employers and employees for example. In Czechoslovakia the situation was quite different. A few persons had become such powerful symbols of the country's unity that the attack had to concentrate on them. Socio-economic groupings played no discernible role (until much later when students and workers seemed to continue some form of opposition long after the middle class had yielded). In the early weeks of the resistance it was not so much groups of people which were split from one another as two idealised images which were gradually becoming incompatible: one was the idealisation of the resistance as an uncompromising defiance of the occupant; the other the idealisation of the leaders as symbols of the resistance . These two perceptions of the situation became incompatible because the leaders were openly accommodating and compromising with the occupant. The resulting ideological ambiguity sapped the force of the resistance at its core and effectively split the leaders from the masses, although the ambiguity itself prevented a complete realisation of the fact. This extensive reliance from the outset on intrinsically vulnerable symbols (as leaders are), a reliance which could not subsequently be dispensed with without precisely endangering the unity of the resistance, was undoubtedly one of the weakest links in the chain in Czechoslovakian resistance.

In the first phase of the war, it was noted, the forces of the resistance must all be directed to the goal of protecting the centre of gravity. Achieving this is the one, unique criterion by which the methods of Chapter II and the organisational forms of Chapter III are to be judged (ignoring here their possible bearing on dissuasion prior to invasion and on the counter-offensive — the latter of which is dealt with later).

It is at once apparent that with the methods of Chapter II what matters is the symbolic function (this function being defined in Chapter II in terms of the effects on the resistance itself). The idea of engaging in non-cooperation for the sake of denial, and the idea, particularly, of denying the enemy his 'purpose' (in the above meaning) figure prominently in the literature on civilian defence. This it is now apparent must be rejected as an activity which is generally quite irrelevant. In so far as it is irrelevant it is even dangerous because if it succeeds, nothing is gained, and if it fails the psychological costs may be great. Non-cooperation is useful in two ways: on the one hand it is a form of collective action and as such it has a symbolic value; but then this value is not intrinsically greater than that of other forms of collective action, and where there are no decisive advantages on this count, the likelihood of successful application must be the main consideration in determining which of various alternative actions to chose. On the other hand non-cooperation (and denial in general) may sometimes be useful as a device for denial *per se*, but then not for denying the enemy his *purpose*, but for denying him useful means towards the *aim* (disrupting the unity of the resistance). As noted previously it is not necessary (in the general case) to deny access to the purpose. Clearly, denial has a much less important role to play than is generally assumed.

It is also clear that the undermining functions (splitting, and weakening the opponent) of the methods of Chapter II relate to the counter offensive and are not of primary importance in the initial, predominantly defensive phase. Their crucial importance in the counter offensive will become clear later.

Unity, as we saw in the discussion of the options at the disposal of the occupant, is not just a matter of standing shoulder-to-shoulder. It may take different forms which are not similarly resistant to attack. The unity flowing from intense reliance on a few leaders seems particularly vulnerable. An ideology, which instead of the excellence of leaders and individuals, emphasises the people as a whole and its unity as the true basis of strength seems much more likely to be able to resist the occupant's efforts at disruption. In devising methods with an essentially symbolic aim such distinctions may profitably be kept in mind. As noted in Chapter III there is a tendency in most of the literature on non-violence to see the role of leaders as primarily symbolic (providing an example of courage and firmness) and to attach little importance to their role in strategic planning. This appears on the basis of the discussion in this chapter to be a grave mistake from every point of view. It is not heroism *per se* which is needed, but flexibility by the leadership in adapting to those forms of resistance which the population can sustain and is willing to sustain under the given conditions.

These points about non-violent resistance should suffice to show that the abstract principles developed previously do provide concrete answers when applied to concrete problems, and that they are helpful when it comes to devising a strategy instead of simply drawing up a catalogue of things one could do when attacked. Abstract principles are also helpful in that they show where further elaboration is required. But it is doubtful whether there is much value proceeding further than has been done here, for one soon reaches the limit of what can usefully be said on the basis of abstract reasoning. A correct strategy for a specific struggle must rest on two pillars: general theoretical analysis, and a detailed study of the facts of the case: of the nature of the antagonists, of their 'weapons' and resources, and of the 'topography' of the 'theatre of war'. To build on either alone is another sure path to disaster.

3. THE COUNTER-OFFENSIVE

While the centre of gravity of the defence is determined fairly unambiguously by the general characteristics of non-violent defence and could therefore be discussed in fairly abstract terms, the second centre of gracity, that involved in the counter-offensive, is not so easily specified. This is so because it depends in some measure on the means used in the offence and these may vary considerably from case to case. A precise specification of this second centre of gravity presupposes an analysis of the details of each particular confrontation. Moreover, the offensive means may change to some extent in the course of the struggle and so may therefore may the corresponding centre of gravity.

Here only one particular case will be considered; that in which repression in the form of physical violence is being used against the resistance, whatever the reason, whether to split it or simply in the hope of threatening it into submission. There is not much reason to believe that physical repression would play any major role in practice. In Czechoslovakia it did not occur on any significant scale and the previous analysis suggests that it is probably too crude a means to be of much use to the offence Nevertheless in a theoretical discussion of the feasibility of non-violent defence against military attack it is of course necessary to consider the possibility that it may occur, since it is the main 'resource' which the specifically military character of the attack confers on the attacker.

As with every other act in war, repression is not and cannot be merely a senseless act of wreckage. It is a purposeful act, even if it may be so, only in terms of some weird and misconceived logic. Repression occurs in a particular social, political, cultural and ideological context in which it somehow appears justifiable and appropriate. Conceivably it may be a sheer act of revenge, but even so its limits are set by the political and cultural context in the widest sense. Physical repression can therefore not be conceived of as a wholly arbitrary act, an act which is always "possible in principle", and which is only limited by the physical means available and the humaneness or lack of sufficient motive of enemy leaders.

NON-VIOLENT DEFENCE IN STRATEGIC THEORY

One cannot divorce the 'psychology' and technology of repression from its politics and sociology without severing at the same time all links with reality.

Seen in its proper context, the threat of physical violence as well as its execution is therefore not arbitrary and unlimited but circumscribed by certain inhibiting factors. These factors are not given once and for all. They depend, among other things, on the character of the confrontation between the belligerents, since, for example, violent resistance makes violent repression more acceptable culturally, and hence more feasible politically. Even if the limits thus set may be ill-defined and ill-known, the magnitude of the threat is therefore in principle predictable and in some measure controllable by the resistance. This introduces certain possibilities of a strategy based on the deliberate manipulation of these inhibiting factors.

The centre of gravity for the counter-offensive is constituted by those political, ideological and other factors which ultimately determine the enemy's ability to pursue the offence, and, in the case we are considering, the repression which goes with it. The precise character and relative importance of these factors, and hence the points at which the counter-offensive must be aimed, varies of course from case to case. Generally these factors operate at three points: the local executioners of repression (troops), the domestic political base of the enemy leaders, and the international alignments on which they may depend. It should not be assumed, as there is a tendency to do in much of the literature on non-violence, that the best point of application when it comes to the domestic base of enemy leaders is necessarily public opinion. This may be an important factor to aim at in a country such as the United States where policy is relatively sensitive to public attitudes and information relatively open, but in other cases, as also in that one, rivalries within the political elite, strains within the army, etc. may often be better targets.

Generally, the task is to exploit those strains and contradictions which the act of occupation and the struggle themselves generate within the enemy camp, for it is these which are most readily manipulable by the resistance. These strains may manifest themselves in a variety of ways and they change in the course of the struggle. They may for instance take the form of ideological incompatibilities between self-images of peacefulness and righteousness, and the realities of occupation and repression, between the ostensible purposes of the occupation and its actual effects, and so forth. Reactions in America and abroad to the war in Vietnam provide countless examples, and also illustrate the general proposition stated above, namely that provided it can hold out, time is necessarily on the side of the defence, as these strains and divisions go on widening with time, and this in large measure irrespective of whether the struggle is escalated or de-escalated. How much such contradictions change from one war to another becomes clear when one compares Vietnam with the occupation of Czechoslovakia. Here the ideological conditions which could be exploited were entirely different and gave to certain groups and institutions (such as Czechoslovak workers and the Communist Parties in Czechoslovakia and abroad) a particularly important role in creating and exposing the contradictions of the enemy. Had it been possible to go on tearing at these wounds the occupation could hardly have continued in the long run. Without a closer analysis of the specific conditions of a given conflict the centre of gravity of the counter-offensive can probably not be specified with greater precision than it is in Mao Tse-Tung's formulation: 'the internal contradictions in the enemy camp'. It is these which must be deepened and exploited.

It may seem that we are here getting far away from one of the fundamental principles of Clausewitzian strategy: the separation of war and politics, of aim and purpose, and that strategy as we are here using the term merges into politics. That is not the case. It is politics, culture and ideology which are becoming weapons in a fully Clausewitzian sense. To act on the contradictions – the internal brakes in the enemy camp – is not an act of policy but of strategy, an act of warfare, properly understood. It does not arise from some independent political purpose but is, as must be all action in war, the overthrow of the enemy. The relation between means and purpose is mediated by the aim, as it always is in war, properly conducted. What happens is that in this way the 'strategic space' is expanded well beyond what is traditionally conceived of as the 'theatre of war', but it is still governed by the general rules of strategy.

Action on these political and other 'brakes' is a genuine strategic move in the Clausewitzian sense. It relies upon one's own 'forces' and exploits the weaknesses of the enemy. Whether these are lines which can be outflanked, inadequate supplies, or cultural norms and internal dissensions which block his possibilities of action, makes no difference. Clausewitz constantly refers to 'human factors' as resources in war, and explicitly recognises such immaterial objects as 'unity of interests' and 'public opinion' as possible centres of gravity, hence as suitable points of attack by military or by other means. It is therefore a misunderstanding to conceive of non-violent defence (in the 'negative' mode) as 'putting oneself at the mercy of the enemy' and 'appealing to his conscience'. The inhibiting factors to be exploited are not the good feelings of the enemy (in strategy one always assumes that they are non-existent) but external factors over which the enemy has little or no control, but on which the resistance has a certain influence. The tendency to emphasize conversion as a change of mind and appeals to conscience as a change of heart in the enemy which were noted in Chapter II, therefore seems to be misplaced (in negative non-violence). Devices such as 'amplification of suffering' could be of some use, but then for rather different reasons. Similarly the laboratory experiment by Shure and associates which was described in Chapter II and which suggested that non-violence had no significant effect on the enemy is perhaps of some relevance in relation to positive non-violence, but not in relation to non-violence in the negative conception, for it deals exclusively with 'psychological' effects in individuals which are completely divorced from their social context and which therefore are subjected to no constraints.

From a purely strategic point of view, i.e. disregarding the moral issues involved, the specific utility of non-violence as compared with other means of defence lies in its double function of at once giving rise to a wide range of 'contradictions' in the ideological fabric of the enemy camp, and at the same time denying the enemy the justification, the ideological licence for violence, which a violent response would have provided. These are of course only the two sides of the same coin. The more the enemy resorts to violent repression, the more he widens the contradictions in his own camp until he either reaches a limit beyond which he cannot go, or else, in Clausewitz' words, his 'extreme effort would be wrecked by the opposing weight of forces within itself.' As time passes and contradictions widen, the enemy's tolerance for conducting repression steadily declines.

The utility of non-violence as such is therefore primarily to be found in the counter-offensive. In the defensive phase, what counts in general strategic terms is the popular character of the resistance. Indeed, in considering the first centre of gravity we did not in any way make use of its non-violent character. This is not to deny that in practice this aspect may be important even in the defence, but it is so essentially to the extent that it is a pre-condition for maintaining unity and it thus depends on the specific ideological conditions in each case. In resistance against a military coup, for instance, non-violence appears to be virtually a necessity because the inhibitions against firing 'army upon army' are so great. On the other hand there would be no point in using violence unless it can actually be expected to contribute to unity (as noted in Chapter IV this cannot in all cases be excluded *a priori*).

From the point of view of strategic reasoning it is therefore clear that one cannot argue a general case for non-violence. There may be other factors than the ideological ones which are much more readily exploitable. To put it differently: non-violence seeks to do two things: on the one hand it so organises the defence as to leave as little scope as possible for the use of the enemy's military force; on the other hand it seeks to achieve the attrition of these forces mainly at the ideological level. But a physical attrition of these forces, when it is relatively slow as in guerrilla warfare, may be compatible with retention of the ideological advantages, and may yet be possible without offering any substantial target for the enemy military forces. No abstract reasoning could show that either non-violence or guerrilla warfare is in all cases the most effective. That question can only be settled in each particular case, taking due regard to its specific conditions. It is however clear that in the general context of a non-violent defence, sporadic violence is wholly counter-productive in that it lifts the restraints on the enemy's use of violence without achieving anything worthwhile in return. There is no gliding transition between guerrilla strategy and non-violence: intermediate courses of action are generally worse than either of them.

To show that non-violent defence is a perfectly consistent application of classical strategic theory one last point needs to be considered, which relates to the unity of the strategic field as a whole: the relation between the centres of gravity, and between these on the one hand, and, on the other hand, the purpose of the war. In the simplest case of military force against military force, the symmetry of means suffices to ensure that unity. Consider two armies disputing a certain territory (the purpose). The two centres of gravity lie in these two armies respectively, in their survival as meaningful fighting forces. It is then immediately clear that the destruction of one centre of gravity automatically ensures the survival of the other and is the necessary and sufficient condition for the appropriation of the purpose (on anything but a temporary basis). In the much more complicated and highly asymmetrical case of non-violent resistance against military force these simple relationships cannot be taken for granted.

What needs to be shown in each particular case is that as long as the unity of resistance is not broken the resistance can go on, and as long as this is the case the counter-offensive (deepening contradictions in the enemy camp) can continue so that the possibility remains that the enemy will ultimately be forced to withdraw. This is not always the case (Clausewitz notes the obvious general exception which arises when the purpose is an 'easily removable' object), but where it does apply, consistency is ensured, for the offence will then have to attack the centre of gravity of the defence. Then the separation of aim and purpose is possible; the reciprocal relation of polarity (in Clausewitz' sense) between the centres of gravity, whereby the destruction of one is the necessary and sufficient condition for the preservation of the other is then ensured; and the identification of the aim with this pair of centres of gravity is necessary, in the sense that it is objectively imposed on both belligerents. In other cases, as was noted previously, the defence would have to be specifically designed to protect the purpose.

4. STRATEGY AND DEFENCE IN THE NUCLEAR AGE

It follows from the preceding analysis that non-violent defence, in the form in which it has been presented in this book (i.e. in its negative, pragmatic form) satisfies the general requirements which make it a strategy in the classical, Clausewitzian sense. It may run into any number of problems in actual implementation, and some of these have been discussed in previous chapters, but theoretically it belongs on a par with all other Clausewitzian strategies. Its theoretical foundations are solid.

Clausewitzian theory is a strategic theory because within it, all strategies serve to achieve the same aim: the overthrow of the enemy. They can therefore all be compared in terms of their efficiency. In practice war is such a complex phenomenon and involves so many imponderable factors and chance elements that theory can never hope to become a perfect calculus to determine precisely the best strategy. But in principle there is in each particular case one strategy which is 'better' than all others. Theory can at least help to identify it.

Since Clausewitzian theory establishes a hierarchy among all the strategies which are applicable to a particular conflict, two questions immediately arise: first, are there any defence policies which are not Clausewitzian strategies, and which are therefore incommensurate with the latter. If so, which? Second, what is the complete range of Clausewitzian strategies in the case, say, of a small industrialised country faced with a threat from a major nuclear power? Is there a spectrum of such strategies, and if so which among them would appear, on theoretical grounds, to be the most effective?

For a country which faces a threat by a nuclear power there are indeed 'defence options' which are not Clausewitzian strategies. One is to surrender whenever the enemy issues a threat. Another is to respond to threats with a counter-threat of nuclear reprisals, thus establishing a so-called 'balance of terror'. The latter is obviously not a Clausewitzian strategy, for in the 'balance of terror' virtually all the assumptions of classical strategic theory are violated. War becomes a senseless act, not an instrument of policy. It is not a struggle carried to the extreme but is on the contrary totally dominated by the endeavours of both belligerents to *avoid* the extreme. The belligerents are not in polar opposition to one another but have overriding common interests, and the aim cannot be the overthrow of the enemy or his submission since that would be to court suicide. Finally, in Clausewitzian theory moderation in war and, indeed, peace itself which, to Clausewitz, is like a pause in war, become possible because of the ultimate superiority of the defence over the attack. In other words, peace is rendered possibly by the *strength* of the defence; in the 'deterrence theory' on the other hand, it is claimed that it is precisely the weakness of defence due to the total vulnerability of each antagonist which ensures peace, and moderation in war.

NON-VIOLENT DEFENCE IN STRATEGIC THEORY

In the 'deterrence theory' nuclear weapons come to appear as absolute, ultimate weapons in comparison with which all other weapons are dwarfed. The nuclear weapons alone become strategically decisive.

In this situation one is dealing with a case of 'non-antagonistic' conflict, rather similar to that which was called the 'positive' view of conflict. As mentioned briefly in the introduction, the conflict model associated with positive non-violence has a certain similarity with great-power confrontation under conditions of nuclear deterrence. Despite the quite dissimilar underlying philosophies these two cases give rise to analogous 'strategic' situations. With nuclear deterrence the situation is that of a two-player coalition against a third party, this third party being a non-calculating player and which represents the possibility of common nuclear annihilation. Only in a second approximation is this coalition overlaid with a minor, purely antagonistic conflict which divides the coalition partners over some comparatively unimportant stake. This is of course a non-Clausewitzian situation (as is that of positive non-violence) because the antagonists no longer have any clearly definable interests. They tend to fuse, for when one threatens the enemy he also threatens himself, so that logically speaking it is as though he belongs to both camps at once. Both 'players' become so schizophrenic and all of their actions so ambiguous that there is no longer anything like a 'best' course of action. All that 'deterrence theory' can do is to list the possible courses of action, but it cannot weigh them. It is inherently non-prescriptive.

Deterrence policies arise from, or assume meaning, only within a framework where the acts of the enemy are conceived of as essentially arbitrary acts. Nuclear attack is seen as being always 'possible in principle' if the enemy so chooses. It is an act of his free will, limited only by his technical means and by his calculation of the consequences. This is the intellectual frame in which the 'push-button war' is the enemy and becomes a 'decision-maker' with all the arbitrariness in choice which this expression implies. Because its use is always 'possible' the atomic weapon becomes the arbiter of all confrontations, and as such the absolute weapon, the decisive weapon of ultimate recourse.

The policies of deterrence build on assumptions which are rather suspect in that they conceive of the 'decision situation' in

175

terms of individual psychology. Not that it is demonstrably wrong to do so — threats of reprisal may obviously be effective in some cases (though it is not easy to tell in advance) — but it is a very limited perspective. As a 'theory' of the factors determining the use or non-use of nuclear weapons, it is so narrow that it restricts the range of available counter-measures unduly. This is so because it is an 'abstract theory' in the worst sense. It does not consist in abstracting from superfluous and confusing details to get a clearer view of the whole, but it abstracts from the whole, it completely disregards the political purpose and the political context of real war (and war of nerves), to get a supposedly better view of a little corner: the 'psychology' of 'decision-makers'. By thus divorcing the nuclear threat from its context, that threat inevitably comes to appear as an arbitrary abstract, limitless and omnipresent threat. Moreover, one starts in this way with an assumption about where strategy should find its point of application (namely, in the mind of the 'decision-maker' — compare on this point too with positive non-violence and its reliance on conversion of the enemy). But this was precisely the question in need of an answer. Subsequently deterrence theory remains prisoner of that initial assumption of having started with the answer not the question, and everything is reduced to 'psychology'. For instance the entire debate between doves and hawks becomes a debate over imponderables such as the enemy's ultimate reasonableness and good intentions (implying the utility of arms control and tension reduction) or the enemy's lack of these desirable qualities (implying the necessity of hard-line deterrence and maximum preparedness).

Yet it is only in the lofty abstractness of 'deterrence theory' that one can thus divorce the psychology and technology of the nuclear threat from its sociology and politics. In complete analogy to what has been said about repression, nuclear threats and nuclear attacks are not the unconstrained and arbitrary acts of 'decision-makers'. In the real world they emerge out of a political and cultural context in the widest sense; they have to be imaginable and to seem appropriate and useful, and not only to the issuer of threats or those who implement it. The use of the nuclear threat being thus necessarily circumscribed and at each particular moment limited to some level short of all-out destruction, the nuclear threat therefore ceases to be an absolute threat. So-called nuclear blackmail, however logical and possible it may appear 'in principle', becomes a thing one can resist, even without being a nuclear power or sheltering behind one. And because it becomes relative, the nuclear threat does not necessarily have to be responded to in kind. In fact, if it is assumed that inhibitions of a political, social and cultural nature are normally more decisive in holding back the hand on the nuclear trigger than is fear, then a policy responding to threats with counter-threats becomes nothing less than disastrous, for no policy is more likely to weaken those inhibitions. Instead of a symmetric response, countering like with like, an asymmetric one comes to seem most appropriate.

Thus different assumptions about what it is which ultimately determines the magnitude of the nuclear threat give rise to quite divergent policies.

It has been repeatedly stressed that a weapon *per se*, separated from the context in which it is employed, is an utterly meaningless abstraction. It is no wonder that such conceptions should flourish today when vast investments are made in military hardware which is supposed to frighten by its mere existence, rather than show its value in actual combat, but it is a misconception all the same. A piece of equipment only becomes a weapon when it is given a place in a particular strategy, and only then does it become a useful instrument or a piece of worthless paraphernalia, or even a boomerang. This is as true of nuclear weapons as of any other weapon. Nuclear weapons are absolute weapons in a context of bilateral nuclear confrontation, not in other contexts.

The case of Vietnam may serve to illustrate this. Throughout, the use of nuclear weapons by the American forces has been virtually unconceivable. It has been so, not because there was a risk of nuclear reprisal by the Soviet Union or China — that risk was probably always exceedingly small — but because such an act would lie far outside the limits set by political, social and cultural factors. True, the risk that they may be used, if vanishingly small, is nevertheless not absolutely zero. But *if* they were used, as is 'logically possible', this would be completely self-defeating, as the aggressors' camp would be wrecked by its internal divisions. There is a small risk of sheer madness, but it is strictly a risk of madness, not a risk that the enemy may employ a more effective weapon to improve his prospects of victory. The American nuclear weapons are therefore *strategically* unimportant. They are

WAR WITHOUT WEAPONS

in this context a 'paper tiger'. But the possibility that they may be used is not absolutely nil and therefore these weapons must be taken into account *tactically*. This is all the more essential because the impossibility of using them strategically (i.e., to further the 'aim' of war) is not an *a priori* fact but is entirely dependent upon the specific form the struggle takes. The factors which inhibit their use in a way like that of Vietnam are the *relatively* limited use of violence which takes place on the battlefield, the specific conditions of international alignments and of political strains within the United States itself, and the fact that the counter-offensive proceeds by 'stings' and does not threaten the American homeland, only the forces which penetrate enemy territory. Thus the uselessness of the nuclear weapons depends on the specific conditions throughout the strategic space: the field of battle as well as the political sphere, domestic and international. These particular conditions must be preserved and extended by deliberate action since it is precisely the constraints arising out of these conditions which keep the nuclear risk limited. As a nuclear weapon is not an absolute weapon *per se,* it is also not a 'paper tiger' *per se.* It is only devoid of strategic importance *provided* it is taken fully into account tactically. It is only by adapting one's entire strategy to the fact of its existence, i.e., to the conditions of the nuclear age, that one can turn the nuclear weapon into a 'paper tiger'.

The main features of a strategy designed to achieve this have already been considered, for it is essentially a special case of strategies designed to limit the possibility of repression. It is a strategy where the counter-offensive lies at the political level — acting on the internal constraints in the enemy camp. As regards the forces in the field it is a strategy of dispersal (denying the enemy a worthwhile target) and of interpenetration (using the enemy's forces as hostages to prevent the use of weapons of mass destruction). It is a strategy which makes maximum use of the defence's superiority in respect of time by subdividing battles into small, local and autonomous confrontations, which are too small, too brief and too unpredictable to allow the use of large-scale weapons. Most important of all it is a strategy which refrains from threatening the enemy's homeland physically, since that would be the certain way to bring down the inhibitions against the enemy's use of massive repression, nuclear or otherwise, and to turn the

178

'logical' possibility of nuclear attack into a *real* possibility.

This asymmetrical type of strategy is of course the general method for coping with an enemy which is militarily superior. Guerrilla strategy and the strategy of non-violent defence both belong in this category, the latter being merely a purer form, a more extreme and consistent application of the general principles which also apply to the former. The parallels between guerrilla warfare and non-violent defence which have been noted at several points in this book arise from their common character of being defence methods against an enemy with, relatively speaking, unlimited means of repression. It is reflected in the fact that in both cases the centre of gravity corresponding to the counter-offensive is the same: 'the internal contradictions in the enemy camp'. The differences between these strategies are reflected in the fact that the centres of gravity associated with the defence differ in these two cases (which in turn reflects the different social, artificial and natural conditions under which one or the other is more applicable). In one case this centre of gravity lies in the unity of resistance, in the other it lies in the political mobilisation of the 'masses' for a specific political programme, not necessarily of the people in its entirety. In a confrontation with a nuclear power where one uses a *symmetric* policy (deterrence), nuclear weapons take on an absolute character. When these *asymmetric* strategies are used these weapons become instruments of repression, not substantially different from others, only much more destructive and with a greater moral opprobrium attached to them, and therefore rather less useful than 'conventional' means of repression.

In contrast to the symmetric policies, the asymmetric strategies are fully Clausewitzian. It is only if all-out nuclear war is a real possibility and if the steps leading to it can be rationalised as purposeful policies, (i.e., solely in the case of a bilateral nuclear confrontation), that the common interests of the belligerents come to dominate in such a way that the basic assumptions of classical strategic theory cease to apply. In a confrontation where only one side posesses nuclear weapons there is no community of interest between the belligerents which is in any way different from that which may apply in classical strategy as a result of the subordination of war to policy. Both sides can pursue their own interests singlemindedly and nothing tempers the polarity between them. War may be too costly, in which case the opponents will refrain from it (or, if they do not, will break down internally), but war is not inconceivable, not pure madness as it is with deterrence policies. It remains a purposeful act.

Strategy in the asymmetric case remains Clausewitzian, but there the analogy with pre-nuclear strategy ends. The 'theatre of war' is a wholly different one, politics and culture have become weapons, and the relative symmetry between the means used by both belligerents (which is on the whole characteristic of warfare before the advent of nuclear weapons) disappears. While they do not in themselves constitute an absolute and ultimate weapon, nuclear weapons are certainly important. They are not decisive *in* strategy, but they are decisive *for* it. No previous advance in weapons technology has had such profound implications for the *form* of war and the *form* of strategy. But to see them as spelling the end of defence, the end of war and the end of classical strategy is a mistake. It arises from the tendency to see war and defence in purely military terms, as the exclusive business of soldiers, and from applying to one age, strategic concepts which properly belong to an earlier one. It would be a complete misreading of strategy to assume that military weapons must necessarily be countered with military weapons. Particularly with nuclear weapons, the advantages of countering with different means are glaringly obvious.

Summing up, it appears that apart from the obvious possibility of yielding to such threats as may occur, there are two general categories of possible responses for a country facing a threat from a nuclear power: one is the set of *symmetric policies* which involve deterrence, counter-threat and balance of terror. By adopting such policies the nuclear risk becomes not one of heavy destruction only, but also a risk of complete mutual annihilation. Such policies may work. They sometimes do, as in the Cuban crisis. They may also fail. They lie completely outside the realm of strategy and therefore do not, as do Clausewitzian strategies, provide assurances that gains will not be less than a certain minimum and losses not more than a certain maximum. These policies are essentially a gamble and are so in two ways: first because costs and benefits are not under control, and second, because each time a move is to be made there is no way of deciding in advance which is the better choice. Decisions in 'deterrence strategy' can only be judged in retrospect.

The other set of options consists of the *asymmetric strategies*. They all have a common format and differ in what in this context are details. Non-violent defence is the archetype, the pure case, but is not necessarily the most effective under all circumstances. All these strategies are based on a refusal to threaten reprisals in kind, thus maintaining the nuclear threat at a non-infinite level. The defence may be organised in various ways, but the counter-offensive is in all cases directed against the same centre of gravity. Military means and violence are not *a priori* excluded but if they do occur they do so only at a relatively low level, the lower, the greater the risk of repression, and they are in any case not meant to be decisive. The decision, strategically speaking, lies in the unity and mobilisation of the people on one's own side, and in the disunity and strains on the other side. The decisive battles of the war are political.

These two categories of responses — symmetric and asymmetric — are incompatible, there is no way of chosing a half-and-half course, for one presupposes that nuclear weapons are available, the other that they be discarded. They are also intellectually incompatible because they proceed from different assumptions about the mechanism behind enemy threats, the former building on psychological factors, the latter on socio-political and cultural ones. Furthermore the two categories are incommensurate: deterrence 'strategy' is no strategy; it cannot prescribe any courses of action as being better than others. *A fortiori* it cannot pretend to show that it is superior (or inferior) to non-violence and its analogues. Among the asymmetric strategies it is in principle possible to prove that some are better than others, but this possibility of comparing strategies does not extend beyond those which are Clausewitzian. Classical strategic theory can therefore also not pretend to show that *its* strategies are better (or worse) than the deterrence policies.

Obviously neither category of responses is without risks, but the risks are very different in the two cases. The first is a risk of mutual suicide, the second a risk of conventional or nuclear repression which may be so devastating that political surrender becomes necessary. One can argue indefinitely about the relative likelihood of each.

Even though in the asymmetric strategies the nuclear weapon comes to appear as a 'paper tiger', as not decisive in strategic terms, it would be a complete mistake to think that this arises from an underestimation of its importance or of the vast destruction it can cause. On the contrary, asymmetric strategies are devised in full cognition of the nuclear danger, in the realisation that savage repression is a distinct possibility. Their major concern is to diminish that risk and to block the use of nuclear weapons and any other means of repression the enemy may possess. It is precisely because asymmetric strategies must take full account of the contemporary fact of nuclear weapons that they come to differ so markedly from the primarily military Clausewitzian strategies of earlier times. Neither deterrence nor non-violence ignore the realities of contemporary weaponry. Both seek to cope intelligently with the problem of nuclear weapons, though in very different ways: on their own terms as does the former, or on completely different terms as does the latter.

But this also means that non-violence is something more than an approach to the somewhat parochial, and perhaps even unreal problem of defending the small wealthy countries of Western Europe against hostile Soviet designs. At a deeper level non-violence, like guerrilla warfare and other asymmetric strategies, provides a valid, if not unproblematic, answer to one of the central problems of our age: how to put an end to the hegemony of the nuclear powers, how to annul the nuclear threat by rendering it obsolete and useless. In short: how to leave the nuclear age behind.

WORKS CITED:

Beaufre, André, *Introduction à la Stratégie*, Paris, Armand Colin, 1963.
Bienen, H., *Violence and Social Change*, Chicago, University of Chicago Press, 1968.
Bondurant, Joan, *The Conquest of Violence: The Gandhian Philosophy of Conflict*, London, Oxford University Press, 1958.
Bondurant, Joan, 'Paraguerrilla Strategy: A New Concept in Arms Control', *Journal of Conflict Resolution*, Vol. 7, No. 3, pp.235-245, 1962.
Brandon, H., in *Sunday Times*, London, 23 November 1969.
Bray, H., 'Towards a Technology of Human Behavior for Defence Use', *American Psychologist*, August 1962.
Case, C.M., *Non-violent Coercion: a Study in Methods of Social Pressure*, London, Allen & Unwin, 1923.
Carter, April, 'Advance Preparations for a Civilian Defence Policy' Civilian Defence Conference, Oxford, 1964 (mimeo).
Carter, April, 'Political Conditions for Civil Defence', in *Roberts, 1967f*.
Clausewitz, Carl von. *Vom Kriege*, 17th ed., Bonn: 1966, Dümmless Verlag, 1966. (Abridged version: *On War*, London: Penguin Press, 1968.)
Coser, Lewis, *The Functions of Social Conflict*, London: Routledge and Kegan Paul, 1956.
Crozier, Brian, 'The Strategic Uses of Revolutionary War', *Adelphi Papers*, No. 55, 1969.
Debray, Régis, 'Revolution in the Revolution?' *Monthly Review*, Vol. 19, July/August 1967.
Ebert, Theodor, 'Organisation in Civilian Defence', in *Roberts, 1967f*.
Ebert, Theodor, 'Civilian Resistance in Czechoslovakia: Implications of the August Campaign', *The World Today*, Vol. 25, No. 1, February 1969.

183

WAR WITHOUT WEAPONS

Fanon, Franz, *The Wretched of the Earth*, New York, Grove Press, 1966.

Farmer, J., *Freedom — When?* New York, Random House, 1965.

Fauvet, J.. and Plancharst J., *La Fronde des Généraux*, Paris, Arthaud, 1961.

Galtung, Johan, 'Pacifism from a Sociological Point of View', *Journal of Conflict Resolution*, Vol. 3. 1959, No. 1, pp.67-84.

Galtung, Johan, *Notes on the Balance of Power*, Oslo: Institutt for Samfunnsforskning, Report No. 1-1, 1962 (mimeo).

Galtung, Johan, 'On the Meaning of Non-violence', *Journal of Peace Research*, No. 3, 1965a, pp.228-257.

Galtung, Johan, 'Mot et Nytt Forsvarsbegrep', *Pax*, No. 1, 1965.

Galtung, Johan, 'The Strategy of Non-military Defence', Oslo, Institutt for Fredsforskning, Report No. 20-6, 1967 (mimeo).

Gandhi, Mohandas K., 'Theory and Practice of Non-violence', in *Non-violence in Peace and War*, Vol. 1, Ahmedabad, Navajivan, 1942 (ref. 1931).

Giap, Vo Nguyen, *People's War, People's Army*, New York, Praeger, 1962.

Gleditsch, Nils Petter, 'Educational Preparations for a Civilian Defence Policy', Civilian Defence Conference, Oxford, 1964 (mimeo).

Gleditsch, Nils Petter, 'Non-military Defence as a Strategic Deterrent', Oslo, Institutt for Fredsforshning, 1965a (mimeo).

Gleditsch, Nils Petter, 'Ikke-voldsforsvar som Stategisk Avverge', *Pax*, No. 1, 1965a.

Gleditsch, Nils Petter, *Kamp uten Våpen*, Pax Forlag, 1965c.

Glucksmann, André, *Le discours de la guerre, 1969* Paris, L'Herue, 1969.

Goodspeed, D.J., 'The Coup D'Etat', in *Roberts, 1967f*.

Gregg, R., *The Power of Non-violence*, New York, Schocken, 1966. (2nd revised ed.)

Grimm, *Vom Ruhrkrieg zur Rheinlandräumung*, Hamburg, Hanseatische Verlagsanstalt, 1930.

Guevara, Ernesto, *On Guerrilla Warfare* (H.C. Peterson ed.) New York, Praeger, 1961.

Gwynne-Jones, A., 'Forms of Military Attack', in *Roberts, 1967f.*

Hašek, Jaroslav, *The Good Soldier Schweik*, London, Penguin, 1965.

Holst, Johan J..*et al.*, 'Ikke-militært Forsvar og Norsk Sikkerhetspolitikk', Oslo, Forsvarets Forskningsinstitutt, Tednisk Notat S-142, 1967 (mimeo).

Horseburgh, H. J. N., *Non-violence and Aggression: A Study of Gandhi's Moral Equivalent of War*, London, Oxford University Press, 1968.

Hughan, J. W., *Pacifism and Invasion*, New York, War Resisters League, 1942, abridged ed. in *Sibley, 1963.*

Hutchinson, Royal D., 'Czechoslovakia 1968: The Radio and the Resistance', København, Institute for Peace and Conflict

Research, Report 69-2, 1969 (mimeo).

Janis, Irving L., and Daniel Katz, 'The Reduction of Intergroup Hostility: Research Problems and Hypotheses,' *Journal of Conflict Resolution*, Vol. 3 (1959), No. 1, pp.85-100.

Katzenbach, E. L., 'Time, Space and Will: The Politico-Military View of Mao Tse Tung', in Green (ed.): *The Guerrilla – and How to Fight Him*, New York, Praeger, 1962.

Kennan, George F., *Russia, the Atom, and the West*, London, Oxford University Press, 1958.

Kimche, *Spying for Peace*, London, Weidenfeld and Nicholson, 1961.

King, J. E., 'Strategic Surrender: The Senate debate and the book', *World Politics*, April 1967.

King, Martin Luther, *Why We Can't Wait*, New York, Signet Books, 1964.

King-Hall, S., *Defence in the Nuclear Age*, London, Gollancz, 1958.

Lakey, George, 'Possible forms of Change-over from Military to Civilian Defence', Civilian Defence Conference, Oxford, 1964 (mimeo).

Lakey, George, *The Sociological Mechanisms of Non-violent Action*, in *Peace Research Reviews*, Vol. 2, No. 6, 1968.

Lakey, George, 'Civilian Insurrection', (paper on non-violent insurrections in Guatemala, San Salvador and Chile), Pendle Hill, Pennsylvania, Wallingford, 1969 (mimeo).

Lewis, John, *The Case Against Pacifism*, London, Allen & Unwin, 1940.

Liddell Hart, B. H., *Deterrence or Defence*, London, Stevens, 1960.

Liddell Hart, B. H., 'Lessons from Resistance Movements', in *Roberts, 1967f.*

Lindberg, *et al., Kamp uden Våben*, København, Munksgaard, 1937.

Mao Tse Tung, *Selected Military Writings of Mao Tse Tung*, Peking, Foreign Languages Press, 1968.

Menges, Constantine, 'Prague Resistance 1968, Santa Monica, California, Rand Corporation, Report P-3930, 1968 (mimeo).

Moberg, Erik, 'The Effect of Security Policy Measures: A Discussion Related to Sweden's Security Policy', *Co-operation and Conflict*, No. 2, 1967.

Morgenthau, Hans, 'The Czech Inquisition', *New York Review of Books*, 4 December 1969.

Neal, F. W., 'Coexistence after Czechoslovakia', *War/Peace Report*, January 1969.

Nehru, Javaharlal, *The Discovery of India*, New York, John Day, 1946.

Naess, Arne, 'A Systematisation of Gandhian Ethics of Conflict Resolution', *Journal of Conflict Resolution*, Vol. 2, 1958, No. 2, pp.140-155.

185

Naess, Arne, 'What does Civilian Defence intend to defend?' Civilian Defence Conference, Oxford, 1964a (mimeo).

Naess, Arne, 'Non-military Defence and Foreign Policy', in *Roberts et al.:* Civilian Defence, London, Peace News, 1964b.

Naess, Arne, 'Norge under Okkupasjonen', *Pax,* No. 1, 1965.

Porsholt, Lars, 'Sivil Motstand under Oddupasjon', *Pax,* No. 1, 1965.

Raloff, Karl, 'Ruhrkampen', in *Lindberg et al.,* 1937a.

Raloff, Karl, 'Den Ikke-voldelige Modstand, der Kvalte Kapp-Kuppet', in *Lindberg et al.,* 1937b.

Raser, John, 'Deterrence Research', *Journal of Peace Research,* No. 4, 1966, pp.297-327.

Roberts, Adam, 'Introduction', in *Roberts, 1967f.* (ref. 1967a).

Roberts, Adam, 'Civilian Defence Strategy', in *Roberts, 1967f.* (ref. 1967b).

Roberts, Adam, 'Transarmament to Civilian Defence', in *Roberts, 1967f.* (ref. 1967c).

Roberts, Adam, 'Civilian Resistance in Defence: The Defeat of the Generals' Revolt', in *Vereinigung Deutscher Wissenschaftler, 1967d.*

Roberts, Adam, 'Resisting Military Coups', *New Society,* 1 June 1967e.

Roberts, Adam (ed.), *The Strategy of Civilian Defence,* London, Faber, 1967f.

Roberts, Adam, 'Introduction' to the new ed. of *Roberts, 1967f,* London: Pelican Books, 1969a.

Roberts, Adam and Philip Windsor, *Czechoslovakia 1968,* London, Institute for Strategic Studies, 1969b.

Roberts, Adam, 'A Battle Won, A War Lost', *War/Peace Report,* June/July 1969c.

Ruge, Herman, 'Ikkevoldsforsvar og Moderne Teknologi', *Pax,* No. 1, 1965.

Schelling, T., 'Some Questions on Civilian Defence', in *Roberts, 1967f.*

Schramm, S. (ed. and transl.), *The Political Thought of Mao Tse Tung,* New York, Praeger, 1963.

Sharp, Gene, 'The Meaning of Non-violence: A Typology (revised)', *Journal of Conflict Resolution,* Vol. 3 (1959),No.1, pp.41-66, 1959.

Sharp, Gene, *The Political Equivalent of War: Civil Defence,* New York: Carnegie Endowment for International Peace, 1965.

Sharp, Gene, 'The Techniques of Non-violent Action', in *Roberts, 1967f.*

Sharp, Gene (ed.), 'Defence Without War', Cambridge, Mass. Centre for International Affairs, Harvard University, 1969 (mimeo).

Sharp, Gene, *The Politics of Non-violent Action,* Boston, Porter Sargent, 1973.

Shure, *et al.,* 'The Effectiveness of Pacifist Strategies in Bargaining

WORKS CITED

Games', *Journal of Conflict Resolution,* Vol. 9, 1965, No. 1, pp.106-17.

Sibley, Mulford Q., *The Quiet Battle,* New York: Doubleday, 1963.

Sibley, Mulford Q., 'Pacifism', *Encyclopedia of the Social Sciences,* 1969.

Sternstein, Wolfgang, 'The Ruhrkampf of 1923: Economic Problems of Civilian Defence', in *Roberts, 1967f.*

Sternstein, Wolfgang, 'Gewaltfreiheit und Totalitarismus', in *Vereinigung Deutscher Wissenschaftler, 1967.* (ref. 1967).

Swedish Board of Psychological Defence, *Motståndet i Tjekko slovakien, 1968: Metoder och Erfarenheter,* Psykologistkt försvar No. 44, Stockholm, AB Allmänna Förlaget, 1969.

Thornton, T. P., Terror as a Weapon', in Harry Eckstein (ed.): *Internal War,* New York, The Free Press, 1968.

United Nations, *Report of the Special Committee on the Problem of Hungary,* Supplement No. 18 to the Official Records of the Eleventh Session of the General Assembly, New York, United Nations, 1957.

United States Strategic Bombing Survey, Morale Division, *The Effects of Strategic Bombing on German Morale,* Vol. 1, Chap. 3, Washington, Government Printing Office, 1946.

Vereinigung Deutscher Wissenschaftler, *Wissenschaftliche Arbeitstagung über Civilian Defence: Tagungsbericht,* Bielefeld, Bertelsmann Universitätsverlag, 1967.

Winkler, H.J., 'Die Soziale Verteidigung der Tschechoslowaken: Erste weltgeschichtliche Erfarung mit einer neuen Strategie', *Gegenwartskunde,* No. 4, 1968.

Zeman, Z.A.B., *Prague Spring,* London, Penguin, 1969.

Brief guide to the literature

BIBLIOGRAPHIES:

Carter, April, Hoggett David, and Roberts Adam, *Nonviolent Action: A selected Bibliography*, London, Housmans, 1970.

World Without War Council, *To End War: An Annotated Bibliography and 1968 Literature Catalogue*, California, 1968.

CIVILIAN DEFENCE PROPER:

Roberts, Adam (ed.), *The Strategy of Civilian Defence*, London, Faber, 1967. Revised Penguin edition, 1969.

Roberts, Adam, *et al*, *Civilian Defence*, London, Peace News, 1964.

Roberts, Adam, 'Civil Resistance as a Technique in International Relations', *Yearbook of World Affairs, 1970*, London, Stevens, 1970.

Sharp, Gene, *The Politics of Non-violent Action*, Boston, Porter-Sargent, 1973.

Sharp, Gene, *The Political Equivalent of War – Civilian Defence*, New York: Carnegie Endowment for International Peace, 1965.

American Friends Service Committee, *In Place of War: An Enquiry into Nonviolent National Defence*, New York, Grossman Publishers Inc., 1967.

Galtung, Johan, 'The Strategy of Non-Military Defence', International Peace Research Institute (Oslo), Report No.20-6, 1967 (mimeo).

King-Hall, Stephen, *Defence in the Nuclear Age*, London, Gollancz, 1958.

King-Hall, Stephen, *Power Politics in the Nuclear Age*, London, Gollancz, 1962.

Vereinigung Deutscher Wissenschaftler, *Wissenschaftlich Arbeitstagung über Civilian Defence: Tagungsbericht*, Bielefeld, Bertelsmann Universitätsverlag, 1967.

Sharp, Gene, 'Research Areas on the Nature, Problems and Potentialities of Civilian Defence,' mimeo. Cambridge, Mass.,

BRIEF GUIDE TO THE LITERATURE

Center for International Affairs, Harvard University, 1967.

Wehr, Paul, 'Resistance Communication Under Military Occupation: The Norwegian Experience.' Haverford, Pa., Center for Nonviolent Conflict Resolution, Haverford College, 1971.

'CLASSICS' ON NON-VIOLENCE:

Tolstoy, Leo, *On Civil Disobedience and Non-violence* (selected writings), New York, Bergman Publishers, 1967.

Thoreau, Henri, *On the Duty of Civil Disobedience,* London, Peace News, 1963 (first published in 1849).

Gandhi, Mohandas K., *Non-violence in Peace and War,* Ahmedabad, Navajivan, 1942 and 1948 (2 vols.).

Gandhi, Mohandas K., *Satyagraha: Nonviolent Resistance,* Ahmedabad, Navajivan, 1958.

NON-VIOLENCE, GENERAL:

Miller, William Robert, *Non-Violence: A Christian Interpretation,* London, Allen and Unwin, 1965.

Gregg, Richard B., *The Power of Non-violence,* London, James Clarke, 1960 (first published in 1935).

Case, Clarence Marsh, *Non-violent Coercion: A Study in Methods of Social Pressure,* London, Allen and Unwin, 1923.

Muste, A.J., *Non-violence in an Aggressive World,* New York, Harper, 1940.

Sharp, Gene, 'The Meaning of Non-violence: A Typology' (revised), *Journal of Conflict Resolution,* Vol. 3 (1959), No. 1, pp. 41-66.

Sharp, Gene, *The Politics of Non-violent Action,* Boston, Porter-Sargent, 1973.

Bondurant, Joan, *Conquest of Violence: The Gandhian Philosophy of Conflict,* London, Oxford University Press, 1958.

Sibley, Mulford Q. (ed.), *The Quiet Battle: Writings on the Theory and Practice of Non-violent Resistance,* New York, Double-day, 1963 (anthology).

Lakey, George, *Strategy for a Living Revolution,* San Francisco, Freeman, 1973.

Shivers, Lynn and Theodore Olson, *Training for Nonviolent Action,* Philadelphia, Friends Peace Committee, 1971.

Stiehm, Judith, *Nonviolent Power: Active and Passive Resistance in America,* Lexington, Mass., D. C. Heath, 1972.

Tinker, Jerry, 'The Political Power of Non-Violent Resistance: The Gandhian Technique', *Western Political Quarterly,* Vol. 24, Dec.

Lynd, Staughton, *Nonviolence in America: A Documentary History,* Indianapolis, Bobbs Merrill, 1966.

PACIFISM:

Mayer, P. (ed.), *The Pacifist Conscience,* London, Penguin Books, 1966 (anthology).

189

WAR WITHOUT WEAPONS

Martin, D.A., *Pacifism: An Historical and Sociological Study,* London, Routledge and Kegan Paul, 1965.

TYPOLOGIES AND ANALYTIC WORKS:

Naess, Arne, 'A Systematisation of Gandhian Ethics of Conflict Resolution', *Journal of Conflict Resolution,* Vol. 2 (1958), No. 2, pp. 140-155.

Galtung, Johan, 'On the Meaning of Non-violence', *Journal of Peace Research,* (1965), No. 3, pp. 228-257.

Galtung, Johan, 'Pacifism from a Sociological Point of View', *Journal of Conflict Resolution,* Vol. 3 (1959), No. 1, pp. 67-84.

Galtung, Johan, 'The Strategy of Non-Military Defence' (*supra*).

Sharp, Gene, *The Politics of Non-violent Action* (*supra*).

Lakey, George, 'The Sociological Mechanisms of Non-violent Action', *Peace Research Reviews,* Vol. 2 (1968), No. 6.

Kahn, Herman, 133
Kamikaze, 88
Kapp, Dr Wolfgang, 123ff
Kapp Putsch, the, 117, 122ff
Katzenbach, E. L., 77
Kennan, George F., 79, 145ff
Kimche, 47
King, J. E., 12
King, Martin Luther, 70
King-Hall, Commander Sir Stephen, 8, 13, 45
Krupp, 98f
Krushchev, N., 15

Lakey, G., 22f, 25, 65, 140
League of Nations, 102
Literani Listi, 112
Luttwitz, General von, 123f

Mafia, 85
Mahdi, 88
Mao Tse-Tung, 70f, 77, 79, 150, 163, 170
Mau-Mau, 85
media, communication, 40, 60, 85, 108ff
Menges, C., 103, 108, 110
military coups, 40, 60, 85
Moberg, E., 134
Morgenthau, H., 114

Naess, A., 15, 21, 24, 35, 45f, 49, 61
Napoleon, 17, 156, 161
NATO, 106, 118, 142f
Nehru, J., 70
non-cooperation, 44ff, 145, 166
non-violence: ethical argument for, 11f, 21;
  pragmatic argument for, 12f, 16, 21, 61;

negative view of, 13ff, 21, 23ff, 33ff;
positive view of, 15ff, 21ff, 31ff;
see also defence, civilian
Northern Ireland, 17f
Novotny regime, 106ff
nuclear warfare, 7f, 15, 89f, 128f, 174ff

obstruction, 40ff, 47

pacifism, 37, 50ff
Pallach, Jan, 50
Pavel, 113
Pax, 68
Poincaré, 101
polarisation, 29ff, 36
Politics of Non-Violent Action, 37
Porsholt, L., 137
Pouilly, General de, 120

Quisling regime, 59, 64, 119

Raloff, K.,123f
Raser, J., 132
repression, 56, 62, 70, 82ff, 94, 97, 165, 168ff, 178
resistance: vulnerability of, 55ff, 64f;
  co-ordination of, 58ff, 65f;
  leadership of, 61ff, 66f;
  flexibility of, 64f;
  and guerrilla warfare, 68ff;
  against occupation, 92ff;
  against military coups, 17ff;
  unity of, 106ff, 163ff;
  see also solidarity
revolution, 71